DISRUPTING CATEGORIES, 1050–1250

BOOK CULTURES

Further Information and Publications

www.arc-humanities.org/series/book-series/

DISRUPTING CATEGORIES, 1050–1250

RETHINKING HUMANITIES THROUGH PREMODERN TEXTS

by

ELAINE TREHARNE

ARC HUMANITIES PRESS

British Library Cataloguing in Publication Data
A catalogue record for this book is available from the British Library.

ISBN (Hardback): 9781802700862
ISBN (Paperback): 9781802704457
e-ISBN (PDF): 9781802702897

www.arc-humanities.org

Printed and bound in the UK (by CPIGroup [UK] Ltd), USA (by Bookmasters), and elsewhere using print-on-demand technology.

Publisher (manufacturer) details: Arc Humanities Press, 14 Clifton Moor Business Village, James Nicolson Link, York YO30 4XG, United Kingdom.

EU Authorized Representative details (for GPSR purposes): Amsterdam University Press, Nieuwe Prinsengracht 89, 1018 VR Amsterdam, The Netherlands. www.aup.nl

CONTENTS

LIST OF ILLUSTRATIONS

Please note that images from the British Library have had to be supplied in a format that is less high-quality than desirable. This is because the services of the Library were compromised by a cyber-attack in October 2023, with repercussions that are still ongoing in 2024.

SERIES EDITORS' PREFACE

SINCE THE PUBLICATION of Donald McKenzie's landmark book, *Bibliography and the Sociology of Texts* in 1986, there has been a growing realization by researchers and practitioners of the significance of bookish forms of communication—their wholeness, materiality, contexts of production, and multiple meanings through time and space. This new series, Book Cultures, aims to produce short and focused scholarly contributions to the field of bibliographical, media, and manuscript studies. Our books propose new approaches to technologies of text that contribute significantly to contemporary debates: how can documents, manuscripts, printed books, and contemporary digital platforms and devices be regarded afresh? How can new perspectives on form, genre, multimodalities and multirealities provide innovative interpretations of early, modern, and contemporary textual objects to reveal different ways of understanding and appreciating the surviving historical record and, where relevant, foreground its distinctively handmade qualities? Book Cultures aims to start conversations and highlight innovative and creative thinking about all forms of written and illustrated communication from any period and any global tradition. We invite all scholars to participate in this ongoing discussion.

In this inaugural volume, *Disrupting Categories*, Elaine Treharne offers four British manuscript case studies from the twelfth and thirteenth centuries to highlight fundamental concerns about modern tendencies towards classification through academic focus on disciplines, periods, languages, genres, and palaeographical descriptors. Professor Treharne's significant research output on Early English, Text Technologies, editorial method, and the production of manuscripts culminates here in reflections about the limitations of current approaches to books and text. Her efforts seek to open up these objects of study and inspire arts and humanities scholars to undertake new approaches and methods in their avenues of exploration.

We are deeply thankful to Arc's acquisitions editor, Anna Henderson, for her constant inspiration and patient shepherding of this series and its volumes, and to Arc Humanities Press for this opportunity.

Mateusz Fafinski
Bonnie Mak
Elaine Treharne

ACKNOWLEDGEMENTS

NO SCHOLARSHIP ON medieval literary cultures that uses original manuscript sources can be completed without the assistance and support of librarians, archivists, and digitizers. Through the years of the COVID-19 pandemic especially, manuscript scholars like me (and especially scholars far away from the repositories where their materials are kept) relied on the work of the digitizing, cataloguing, and curatorial teams in libraries internationally in order to maintain any kind of research effort. To the teams at the British Library, those at the Cambridge colleges and its University Library, Oxford's Bodleian Library, the National Library of Wales at Aberystwyth, thank you so very much. Stanford University Library was among the first divisions on campus to reopen after the initial pandemic lockdown in 2020: astonishing professionalism and dedication was shown by all library colleagues to permit readers entry to the library and its collections. Thanks especially to Roberto Trujillo, Benjamin Albritton (thanks, Ben, for all the collaboration and friendship), Timothy Noakes, Astrid Smith, Kathleen Smith, and Rebecca Wingfield. To all digitizing, cataloguing, and curatorial teams in repositories large and small, thank you. I am grateful to my research assistant, Eyup Eren Yurek, for reading through and commenting upon the completed draft of this book.

The reason I stumbled into the twelfth century in the first place as an Early English doctoral student at the University of Manchester was through the influence of my supervisor, Professor Donald G. Scragg (though he tried to drag me back to pre-1100). He died in October 2021, but left the scholarly world so much richer through his range of publications; his brilliant research on Old English textual cultures, early scribes, and manuscripts; and his pioneering work on the history of the English language. I am very grateful to him. I have benefitted over the years from the collaboration and friendship of many medievalist colleagues. It can be the best of communities. I am especially grateful and indebted to Matthew Aiello, Tom Bredehoft, Jayne Carroll, Orietta Da Rold, Jill Frederick, Chris Jones (Utah), Andrew Prescott, Kathryn Starkey, and, as always, Greg Walker. I want to thank Mateusz Fafinski, Bonnie Mak, and our brilliant editor, Anna Henderson at ARC. The anonymous reader for the book was particularly attentive, kindly critical, and they helped me clarify and distil central ideas: thank you so very much. This book, as with everything I have done, could not have been completed without the support of my beloved Andy, Joffy, and Izzy Fryett.

PREFACE

THIS SHORT BOOK will address a set of current critical issues in the study of Early English humanities. It focuses on how scholars define written works as L/literature and history; how humanities departments and disciplines organize their Western medieval objects of study through categories of periodization and language; and how scholarly investigation of manuscripts and scripts privileges taxonomy and clarity, but at a cost to our understanding of these fields of exploration.

Labels like "literature" and "history," inherited from the beginnings of modern university disciplines and fields of study, have long been superimposed onto what might be much more flexible modes of research and scholarship. Categorization, while essential (and especially so for metadata creation and discoverability), can hinder nuance, intellectual nimbleness, and new interpretative possibilities. It is helpful to acknowledge that more explicitly in research and teaching: how limited and limiting a particular perspective might be. The reading of texts and textual objects through genre or period as, say, "fictional" or "legal," "Old English" or "Early Middle English," "*de luxe*" or "ordinary" can mean having to navigate challenging foundational approaches and sources for the respective disciplines of English language, literature, linguistics, religious studies, art history, book historical/media studies, and history that confine and often frustrate scholarly investigation. This happens because inherited categories from genre to period to discipline neither work effectively to represent the textual objects that survive nor encourage more contemporary methodologies that could be beneficially applied to their study. Inter-, trans-, and cross-disciplinarity that emerged as modes of analysis more than a generation ago have had less impact on broadening and enriching fields of study than they might; training, for example, in medieval studies or digital humanities still results in scholars' publishing, employment, appraisal, and promotion processes being filtered through the core disciplines, and all too often work produced in one discipline is not widely read or taken up in another, while work that is striving to be interdisciplinary and broad can be criticized for the privileging of breadth over depth. What new models of exploration or what fresh approaches might be determined? This book illustrates through detailed analysis of four main case-studies the kinds of new information and understanding that can be brought to light, but scholars and teachers might have a myriad of their own ideas about how inherited categories can be productively disrupted, perhaps in ways that can make the humanities more accessible to broader audiences.

As several recent studies have shown,[1] the broad arena of humanities in the academy—especially within Anglophone countries—is in some disarray. There are many contributory factors. Presently, some classics, history, literature, and language departments within small and large universities have been closed or are threatened with closure; in many Higher Education institutions, whole departments have been targeted for elimination for some decades now (music and philosophy, for example, have been among the first to be dissolved; but now languages and literatures are also threatened).[2] Subdisciplines have been eradicated in some places (medieval history at the Australian Catholic University and medieval literature and English language at the University of Leicester, for example); and in the UK, in particular, government and public funding for humanities students at all levels has been reduced to negligible amounts as student numbers are perceived to be in decline and the belief in the importance and efficacy of humanistic study is eroded. While these problems for the humanities are not directly attributable to inherited categories of investigation, it is the case that the battening down of hatches between and within disciplines hinders work that might provide a larger picture underscoring why humanities research and teaching is so fundamental to human experience and endeavour. In addition, and rather bafflingly to a humanist, many students and members of the engaged public do not know what "humanities" actually are; the disciplines involved—philosophy, African studies, American studies, East Asian studies, classics, English, music, art, art history, religious studies, parts of anthropology, history, languages, literature, and others—are not necessarily what audiences imagine by "humanities." On countless occasions, I have been directly asked what is meant by "humanities," or happily told by a student that they are doing a humanities class—in international relations or political science. More troublingly still, the skills associated with being a professional humanist are misunderstood or undervalued; courses in environmental or medical humanities or arts are taught in departments outside

---

1 Most recently and trenchantly, Weiskott's *Meter and Modernity*.

2 There is a great deal of apocalypticism in the press and social media about the doomed humanities, much of it exaggerated and focused on elite institutions. See, among many others, Heller, "The End of the English Major"; Baker, "Arts and Humanities cuts 'endemic'"; and, as a form of response, the British Academy's SHAPE programme.

arts and humanities and may not include a single *professional* humanist with an advanced degree in the subject: someone who makes their living through their subject knowledge. The skills, methodologies, and expertise of the disciplines are ignored and trivialized. This is where humanists must start to protest and insist on a place at the table: reading a book does not make the reader a humanist; humanists are not hobbyists. Many humanists are, though, seeking to make their work accessible and available to broader audiences. Public engagement by, and the social impact of, professional humanists has never been greater, for instance. Many academics, and colleagues who are independent or in academic-related posts, are focusing their energies on producing scholarship aimed at a general audience. Trade books appear apace, museum and library exhibitions are flourishing, and contemporary modes of knowledge transfer (social media, blogs, television programming, podcasts, YouTube videos) are enhancing audiences' experiences of the humanities in all its richness.

Disrupting Categories seeks to contribute to the debate about the value, variety, and openness of humanistic research by way of specific case studies from centuries ago. Through this series of short texts, written between 1050 and 1250, the book will highlight how limiting modern scholarly categories can be and how pertinent studying the past remains for the present and for future research. The four studies will focus on periodization, linguistic siloing, originality and copying, disciplinary framing, and on contemporary narratives that—in insisting on an aesthetic of textual production—do not reflect the lived experiences of medieval writing communities. Each chapter will tackle a medieval text or manuscript that is not particularly well known to suggest that by treating texts as objects of investigation in their own right we might free ourselves from the limitations of labels, genres, and prescribed value judgements. Premodern works and those who manufactured them can be productively and joyfully reappraised and freshly appreciated, both within our respective disciplines, but more importantly *between* them, to create open-ended space for discovery and interpretation.

Introduction

OLD ENGLISH AND ITS AFTERWORD

THIS BOOK CONSISTS of four studies. These explore a selection of medieval texts and manuscripts within their respective moments of production and survey their reception by scholars in the modern era. This introduction will set the scene by discussing how contemporary scholarship has inherited particular categories (that is, forms of understanding), labels, and modes of study that can be reimagined to allow for textual materials like those upon which I focus to be interpreted more fully, appropriately, and sensitively.

English after 1100 and its Scholarly Reception

Until quite recently, introductions to the history of English literature and language or to the English High Middle Ages contained exaggerated statements about the decline of the vernacular textual tradition. These are attributed, for the most part, to the sociopolitical changes brought about by the Norman Conquest in October 1066 and its cultural impact in the generations following, when the French of England became a dominant mode of communication among the aristocracy and educated professional classes, vying for attention with Latin, itself always the language of the church liturgy and highest levels of education.[1] According to this old and mistaken (but still quite frequently expressed) scholarly narrative, English only survived because of its persistence as a spoken language and a clinging to tradition by pockets of users in regions distant from London and other major urban sites.[2]

---

1 Tahkokallio, in the "Introduction" to *The Anglo-Norman Historical Canon*, states in relation to the "rupture of the Norman Conquest:" "As the vernacular languages were not yet (or not anymore, in the case of Old English) available as literary vehicles, many secular aristocrats of the era received education in Latin, often beyond its rudiments."

2 See, for example, McCully and Hilles, *The Earliest English*, 257. "Throughout the post-Conquest period, native 'English' literary production appears to come almost to a standstill"; or Machan, *English in the Middle Ages*, 37: "From the 150 years after the Conquest, comparatively little English of any kind survives"; and the most recent edition of the *Oxford English Dictionary*, "After the Conquest, English became pushed out of these functions [of writing] almost entirely. Latin predominates in most types

Focused publications and projects produced in the last thirty years by a very active cohort of researchers has unequivocally shown that English might have lost some of its centralized authority in the post-Conquest period, but it did not lose its vigour or its status of use for religious, didactic, and pragmatic texts—especially those written in prose. Hundreds of manuscripts survive that can be dated approximately from 1050 to 1250, containing in total thousands of individual literary works written in English.[3] A good proportion of these texts are witnesses of sermons and saints' lives, or laws, or treatises that were composed first in the pre-1050 period and then adapted or recontextualised, modernized and transformed in the twelfth and earlier thirteenth centuries.[4] What do these post-1050 versions become? How are they labelled? One of the principal modern categories or forms of understanding that fails to account for the textual richness of this earlier literary era is the binary of "original" versus "copy." Since the emergence in the early modern period of concepts of "copyright" and "authorship," and the privileging of an ideal of creativity and innovation, the thousands of medieval works that are "copies" of texts written earlier are left out of the literary record and not regarded as worth studying in their own right. They are, effectively, reduced to fragments when they appear as "textual variants" at the bottom of the page of scholarly editions. Little or no attempt is made to interrogate the differences that inevitably occur in the process of writing out a text. Not much merit is attributed to the "copy" as a discrete entity; neither is the "copy" valued for how it might express its own unique intersection of influences. It is worth pointing out quite bluntly that in manuscript culture, when every word is handwritten, when every product is unique, there can be no such thing as a "copy."

It is not just individual texts that are fragmented and downgraded from "literature" to "something less than." The ways in which the academy has divided up the history of English literature and language into periods has resulted in the fragmentation of the story of English and the marginalization of the medieval. For the sake of the arrangement of the academic year, literature and history departments generally divide up their long chronologies of the western canon into course-length chunks; students move on to the next

---

of writing in the immediately post-Conquest period": www.oed.com/discover/middle-english-an-overview.

3 Da Rold, Kato, Swan, and Treharne, *The Production and Use of English*.

4 See Treharne, *Living Through Conquest*; Swan and Treharne, eds., *Rewriting Old English in the Twelfth Century*; Faulkner, *A New Literary History*; Home, *The Peterborough Version of the Anglo-Saxon Chronicle*; Butler, *Language and Community in Early England*.

module when they have completed "The Renaissance" or "Enlightenment America" or "Contemporary Literature," and not all courses are required by entire cohorts of students. My own undergraduate experience at the University of Manchester in the 1980s centred almost entirely around mandatory core courses—including Old English, Middle English, Modern English Language, History of the English Language, Renaissance and Early Modern Literature, Literature 1789–1900 and post-1900 (which I persuaded the Head of Department to exempt me from to take another Old English course)—and then advanced selected topics, like English historical linguistics, or Shakespeare, or palaeography, or art and archaeology. The mandatory literature courses were tackled chronologically, such that one gained a sense of the movement and wide influences of writing and writers. I am grateful I experienced a broad range of canonical literature (and had small seminars with demanding tutors who would comment in written [B+] feedback how easily taken in students are by *Wuthering Heights*, "this silly little book"!). I was lucky to work with Dr. Alexander Rumble on his palaeography courses for two full years. Generally, undergraduates are not so fortunate in having access to such specialist training, and it remains a problem that fields like palaeography or premodern art and archaeology are often regarded not as integral, but as add-ons, to disciplines like English and history. Similarly, as Chapter 2 will show, it is problematic for *literature* to be regarded as a footnote in the study of history.

More problematic, perhaps, is the freedom of choice that many undergraduates have as they make their way through degree programmes in the humanities which may have few prerequisites and requirements. The *choice* is not the problem; the disconnectedness that emerges may be, especially since students themselves are left to make sense of the trajectories of time and space that they cover in their individual programme schedules. The issue of periodization especially has vexed the academy for a while. Ted Underwood traces the emergence of literature courses in contemporary English departments in *Why Literary Periods Mattered*. Underwood argues that "the authority of periodization does not rest on the convenience of boundaries. It springs from a commitment to discontinuity that has long defined the cultural purpose of literary studies, and that contemporary scholars still feel as part of their disciplinary identity."[5] He urges that we take up digital technologies, big data studies, to ask new and more challenging questions of the literary object of study, but this approach, or set of tools and methods, almost always precludes the premodern, as does Underwood's

5 Underwood, *Why Literary Periods Mattered*, 161. In his discussion, Underwood suggests curricula could be "organized around a more properly literary category, like genre" (2). I take up the problem of genre in later chapters here.

book indeed. Underwood comments, too, that "periodization is a by-product of professional specialization," but one could argue that the opposite is true and our specializations perpetuate periodization, when there is no real need for this.[6] Certainly, an academic will find themselves labelled as "the medievalist" or "the Early Americanist," responsible for provision in those particular areas of teaching in literary departments, and obliged to apply for jobs and promotion specifically with those chronological demarcations. So many present-day scholars work productively across chronologies, though, and indeed whole areas—like Medievalism—thrive on the transchronological approach to literature and other cultural products.[7]

As many have pointed out over the last twenty years, Early English (anything pre-1500, essentially) is a fraught, sub-divided area.[8] Mary Rambaran-Olm discusses how periodization (especially in Early English) encourages gate-keeping and reinforces racist and centrist practices, by restricting study to the "English" only, and by insisting on a linear and episodic characterization of time.[9] New work, building on decades of innovative research into identity, politics, and the colonial in medieval scholarship, has exposed the exclusionary practices of medieval scholarship and its tendencies to reinforce established categories of practice.[10] Categories are organizational tools permitting concepts or things to be defined according to shared components or types. They are part of how knowledge systems are arranged, but it is incumbent on scholars to be alert to the assumptions that underpin the use of categories and to be explicit about the perspective that is being deployed. Here, because I seem to think in binaries, this study takes as its groupings of contention a series of common categorical binaries: fiction/fact (which could be interpreted, too, as literature/history), authority/anonymity, original/copy, Old/Middle English, and script/hand/production. Numerous other categories for re-examination exist; these range from

6 Underwood, *Why Literary Periods Mattered*, 2.

7 See, for example, Jones, *Strange Likeness*; Hsy, *Antiracist Medievalisms*; Chaganti, *Strange Footing*; and Tracy, *Why Study the Middle Ages?*

8 Treharne, "Categorization, Periodization"; Rambaran-Olm, "A Wrinkle in Medieval Time."

9 Rambaran-Olm, "A Wrinkle in Medieval Time," 397–99.

10 Notable works examining labels, categories, and modes of description and difference include Heng, *The Invention of Race*; Heng, *The Global Middle Ages*. Foundational studies of categories (as a broad category) are Lakoff, *Women, Fire, and Dangerous Things*; Foucault, *The Order of Things*; and Foucault, *The Archaeology of Knowledge*.

languages/communities/networks to England/Britain/medieval world, or centre/margin/edge, or certainty/probability/speculation.[11]

The earliest English ("Old English," or less accurately or helpfully "Anglo-Saxon"), with its foreign-looking lexis and syntax, is often separated from the English that follows: the University of Cambridge's Department of Anglo-Saxon, Norse and Celtic, for example, is distinct from the *English* Department, whose coverage begins somewhere after 1100. Many departments of English claim to teach "medieval" literature, but their coverage does not begin until Geoffrey Chaucer's works in the late fourteenth century, consigning seven hundred years' worth of earlier English to oblivion.[12] "Medieval" can account for one thousand years of Western European history from ca. 500 to ca. 1500, or it can be restricted in use to the later centuries of this period. English literary history surveys, when comprehensive, begin with "Old English" up to 1066 or 1100, followed usually by "Early Middle English" from 1100 or 1150 up to perhaps 1250 or 1300 or 1350, then "Middle English" up to ca. 1500; "Early Modern" (1500–1800) follows; with "Modern" and "Contemporary" rounding off the chronology. These are divisions convenient for organizational purposes, but not for a complete acknowledgement of the movement of vernacular literature through time. What becomes rather messy and opaque is the status of prose and poetry in precisely the period studied here—ca. 1050 to 1250. The reasons for this are the superimposition of political divides onto cultural production; that is, the end of the so-called "Anglo-Saxon" period in 1066 or—without any justification, 1100—being conflated with claims that works written in "Old" English end then, too. The influence of these political divides has then been unhelpfully overlain upon the evolution of linguistic change to create the transition from Old to Middle English in a falsely temporalized process; that is, Old English to 1100,[13] Early Middle or Middle from that point, as if language forms suddenly switched from one set of morphological or phonological or orthographic options to another at the end of 1099 or 1149. Then, concretizing these imaginary moments of change, scholars, scholarship, and disciplinary sub-fields are labelled by these categories; lectureships in Middle

11 On "England/Britain/Medieval World," see, for example, Wallace, ed., *Europe: A Literary History*; and *Interfaces: A Journal of Medieval European Literatures*.

12 See, for example, the curricula (as of now in 2023) at the Universities of Leicester and Reading in the UK, and Princeton University in the USA.

13 Or 1150, according to the *Oxford English Dictionary*'s https://www.oed.com/discover/middle-english-an-overview.

English are advertised; journals or organizations of "Early Middle English" are formed.[14]

Early Middle English scholars would thus claim works written in English from the beginning or middle of the twelfth century as the central domain of study. The literary texts most focused upon tend to be poems such as *The Grave* (considered here in Chapters 3 and 4), *Poema Morale*, and recently, *The Orrmulum*. These date from around 1170 onwards. The literary material in English that is extant from 1050 to 1250, and which is loosely based on, or adapted from earlier (Old) English exemplars, does not easily fall into any of these imagined periods or the hierarchy that insists on "original" at the top, and often lies beyond consideration by Middle English or, indeed, "medieval" specialists.[15] Until the last couple of decades, too, works created in England in French and Latin were also not considered within the history of English literature, despite these languages clearly being part of a spectrum of linguistic possibility as far as readers and manuscript producers in England were concerned throughout the medieval and early modern periods.[16] Meanwhile, in the study of other European cultures—like Polish or Czech or Croatian—Latin has always been treated as an integral part of the literary history.

The many English prose philosophical, pastoral, and educative texts that are transmitted from the late eleventh to the fifteenth centuries with a clear link to the pre-Conquest period are thought of neither as "Old English" nor "(early) Middle English" and are not conceived of as texts in their own right; that is, as anchored to their specific moments of production. Those who study later English may regard them as antiquarian remnants of a tradition unrelated to what comes later. Such texts cannot easily slot into contemporary generic classification, either. Among the most important innovations of the twelfth century in French, and later in English, is the romance, and there are no later medieval romances that can be shown to derive from Old English predecessors. This is despite the names of some of them suggesting a reliance on pre-Conquest stories, like those of the later English *Athelston*

---

14 The journal, *Early Middle English*, published by ARC Humanities Press, "devoted to English literature, its production, and its contexts ca. 1100–1350," was first published in 2019.

15 *Routledge Companion to Medieval English Literature*, ed. Radulescu and Rikhardsdottir; and *Cambridge History of Medieval Literature*, ed. Wallace.

16 On the French of England, see *The Futures of Medieval French*, ed. Gilbert and Griffin; and *Language and Culture in Medieval Britain*, ed. Wogan-Browne. For a brief account of the many languages and literatures of Britain in the Middle Ages, see Treharne, *Medieval Literature*.

and the *Lai de Haveloc* (English *Havelock the Dane*), or *Waldef*.[17] There is a pre-Conquest romance, though—*Apollonius of Tyre*, recorded in the eleventh-century manuscript, Cambridge, Corpus Christi College, MS 201. This manuscript was compiled in several different centres (probably Worcester, Winchester, and Exeter), and it contains an extensive collection of laws, religious poems, and sermons. It might be a book put together for the general use of an institution, or it could have been compiled for a secular patron, or even as a model education for a king.[18] Yet *Apollonius of Tyre* in Early English was not the text that influenced Shakespeare's *Pericles*, or other later versions of the classical story.

Since the nineteenth century, then, when the lines of English literature and language were drawn, texts that are twelfth century but written in English clearly could not be "Old" English (or "Anglo-Saxon"). Neither, if they are indebted to earlier textual products, could they be the new "Middle" or "Early Middle."[19] The first three chapters of this study will highlight how these categories prevent a more holistic sense of English literary production in the eleventh and twelfth centuries using texts written in English that confound easy delineation.

True or False? Fiction, Non-fiction, Fact

Modern humanists are used to working in categories of textual division centred on "non-fictional" or "factual," and "historical" set as a contrast to "fictional" and "literary." These are forms not just of generic and textual distinction, but also of scholarly methodology informing disciplinary specialization. In her foundational discussion of archival research, Arlette Farge explains the process of unlocking the past through its primary historical sources:

> The desire to understand is a demanding one, and there are as many illusions to tear down as there are requirements to fulfill. The historian cannot be narrator alone; he must also explain and persuade, providing detailed explanations because he knows that contrary ones can always be advanced. The first illusion that must be cast aside is that of the definitive truthful narrative. A historical narrative is a construction, not a truthful discourse that

17 See *Waldef*, trans. Djordjević, Clifton, and Weiss.

18 Atherton, "Cambridge, Corpus Christi College 201 as a Mirror for a Prince."

19 One of the few scholars to address the issue of the fallacy of the gap between Old and Middle English is Anne Savage in her "Old and Middle English: Poetry and Prose." Her discussion is principally centred on poetry in response to Lerer's focus on poetic texts in his "The Afterlife of Old English."

> can be verified on all its points. The narrative must combine scholarship with arguments that can introduce the criteria of truthfulness and plausibility. The poet creates, the historian argues...The historian is not a writer of fables.[20]

Farge is keen to advance the historian's methodology of argument and evidence. She is particularly alert to the potential for multiple interpretations of the same source—the *many* truths that might emerge from events and stories of the past. There is, though, quite the chasm posited between the production of fiction and the imagination, or the fabular, and the act of construction and persuasion that is embodied in the perceived roles of contemporary academic historians and literary critics and creators. However, the further back in time (literary) historians move, the more difficult it is to establish not only what might constitute "truthfulness and plausibility" but also what "truthfulness" was intended by the creator of the medieval text. When the majority of texts produced in premodern England have no known "author," often cannot be dated, and frequently cannot be localized, their intentionality and functionality is difficult to deduce, and much is a matter of informed interpretation. "Truth" becomes an interesting category of investigation. It is easy, for example, for modern scholars to reject the veracity of miracles in a tenth-century saint's life; but if that life were *perceived* unequivocally to be true, how then might we read sensitively and with an awareness of the socio-historical and religious significance of that life's transmission?

Some of the medieval texts in question can be understood to be conceived of as deliberately constructing *history*, which can yet be opened up for other disciplinary approaches. *The Letter of Eadwine*—a short story contained in two Winchester manuscripts dating to the eleventh and twelfth centuries—is the main focus of the first chapter. The two instantiations of this document, usually understood as a writ, are probably copies of an earlier text, composed by an unknown author at some point between ca. 1030 and ca. 1150 in Winchester. It has been read as a forgery and of little significance, but here I read it as a lively and creative representation of an institutional past told through the narration of a fictional monk; it is a short story by any standards. It is an excellent example of how medieval works—even brief ones—can defy easy categorization that forecloses scholarly interest.

Similarly, hundreds of texts, beyond the law codes, charters, and chronicles usually examined by historians can be deployed as simultaneously sig-

20 Farge, *Allure of the Archive*.

nifying history and the imagination. Within English manuscripts there are dynamic, stylistically complex, and unique testimonies to concerns current at the very time of the manuscripts' production, even though their authors are not known.[21] As Chapter 2's main case study—the anonymous English adaptation of Ralph D'Escures's Homily on the Assumption of the Virgin Mary—shows, the vernacular was an important means of transmitting contemporary theological doctrine in and through the mid-twelfth century. This is no mere copy either since it provides fresh evidence for the reception of new sermons and is a major witness to religio-literary composition in twelfth-century English. This, and most English texts written in the eleventh and twelfth centuries, are reworkings of received materials made anew for different audiences. Scribes, through their deliberate and inadvertent editing, compilers through their innovative sequencing of texts, and translators and adaptors through their individual choices all contribute to a rich and functional corpus of works that deserves detailed attention.[22] Present-day scholars cannot impose desires for originality and invention, known and celebrated authorship and "best-sellerness," on a period when those things were not the dominant understanding of textual production and reception. Such misdirection means the omission of entire groups of literary and cultural products. This corpus of English from 1050 to 1250 contains instances that are often reconceived works aimed at edifying the lives of Christian subjects. But it contains important motifs, ideas, characterizations, instructions, fears, and emergent vocabulary that represent the spirit and endeavour of writers who knew the significance of the English vernacular, not only for imagined communities of readers, but also for scholars, theologians, chroniclers, didacts, and poets.

The Order of Script and Writing

English texts from the later eleventh to earlier thirteenth centuries are anything but "disappointingly undistinguished."[23] Just as the prose sermon on the Assumption of the Virgin in Chapter 2 shows the vitality and usefulness of English as a carrier of up-to-date theology and linguistic expression, so *The Grave* and its manuscript context that provide the main focus of my

---

21 For which, see the essays in Swan and Treharne, *Rewriting Old English in the Twelfth Century*; see also, Swan, "Old English Made New"; and Younge, "The New Heathens."

22 As the research of Faulkner, *New Literary History*, and others amply illustrates.

23 Short, "Language and Literature," 194.

attention in Chapter 3 and the opening of Chapter 4 demonstrate the complexity of textual compilation. In this poem and its manuscript, the layered nature of compositional method and form, as well as the piling up of palaeographical and codicological clues, permits a fresh assessment of the motivation and means for manuscript facture from about 1170 to 1220—decades of dramatic transformation in script and the production of writing.[24] Written in a period of significant cultural transition, *The Grave* and Oxford, Bodleian Library, MS Bodley 343 sit between literatures and languages, disrupting the definitional and disciplinary boundaries discussed in Chapters 1 and 2, but also bringing to the fore how much more there is for scholars to research in this period. Chapter 4 calls for a reappraisal of manuscript researchers' thinking on environments of writing and categories and descriptive labels for script. This leads to my questioning of what sometimes passes as evidence in palaeographical analysis, and to a new re-dating of the work of the Tremulous Hand of Worcester.

Scribes, scribal practices, and the locations of scribes come under scrutiny in a reinvestigation of one of the most famous documents in western history—the Magna Carta, and particularly the Salisbury Magna Carta, perhaps the best preserved of the four instantiations of this notable textual landmark from 1215. I question the demarcation of administrative and ecclesiastical centres of production and look again at the evidence for assignment of manuscripts to specific centres and how and why examples of categories of text are judged in the way they are.

Through the case studies in this short book, I raise issues that surround how scholars describe and work with their primary sources as they build on inherited scholarship. None of us can do the research we do without standing on the shoulders of those who precede us, and in deep appreciation of how far we have come in studying premodern textual cultures through specialist categories of investigation, this book thus asks where next, and in what directions we might proceed by modelling open-minded scholarly inquiry into texts that are not usually the focus of sustained attention. I suggest and demonstrate that allowing our textual objects of investigation—the manuscripts, documents, texts, and creators of these—to be perceived on their own terms, as well as being able to speak to other textual objects in multiple systems of knowledge, yields new findings and hints at further exciting avenues of research for Humanists.

---

24 Palaeographical information comes from the handwriting and scribal features; codicological information comes from the physical make up and structure of the book itself.

Chapter 1

FACT AND FICTION

HISTORY AND THE IMAGINATION

THE *LETTER OF EADWINE* is included in two manuscripts that bridge political and cultural upheaval (periodized as pre- and post-Conquest) and regions of medieval England (the north and south). A short and entertaining text narrating the adventures of a Winchester monk, Eadwine, the letter or writ reveals a great deal about how the major religious houses in Winchester and Durham wished to promote their institutions and saints long into the twelfth century. More, this short text is neither history, nor memoir; neither fiction nor epistle; neither romance nor hagiography. It problematizes issues of form, genre, and function, present and past, in a delightful story of care for the body of the long-dead Cuthbert, and the ongoing curation and preservation of relics from days gone by. Present-day scholarly obsessions with chronology and sociopolitics dissipate in a short but complex narrative that fruitfully defies categories.

This chapter considers the use of the past. How was it used in the eleventh and twelfth centuries. How is it used now? And how did manuscript compilers and textual producers in the distant past use their *own* pasts?[1] From this long temporal distance, is it possible to learn more about how and for what purpose institutional author-scribes reinvented their own histories for their own communities? The twelfth-century English work that I call the *Letter of Eadwine* highlights the significance of these questions for post-Conquest English literary production and calls into question the usefulness of present-day disciplinary claims of what constitutes "fact"—the historical—versus the non-historical, the literary, the fictional.

Guilty in some respects of perpetuating the same dividing line between the literary and the historical, in 2005, Mary Swan, Orietta Da Rold and I began a British Arts and Humanities Research Council-funded digital project, *The Production and Use of English Manuscripts, 1060 to 1220*, which ran until 2010, but is still widely accessible and frequently cited. In the design of the project, we made the difficult decision to omit from our database

1 An early version of this chapter was given as a paper at the "Anglo-Saxon Kingdoms" conference in the British Library, London, in December 2018. I am grateful to the audience for their attention and feedback.

of *literary* manuscripts all cartulary and legal materials copied in English during this period.[2] We knew we should be in danger of not finishing the project in the five-year period of the grant if we took these texts into the project in addition to the thousands of "literary" works we did include. Cartularies and single-leaf diplomata (administrative and legal documents) are varied and deeply informative materials, though, and are rich resources for studying the medieval period, containing pertinent information for constructing sociocultural, religious, and materialist histories.

Cartularies can be broadly defined less by their contents and materiality and more by how they function historically and memorially. Although the term derives from the Latin *carta*, a charter (so, loosely speaking, a cartulary might be a book-shaped collection of charters), these manuscripts are often written over long periods of time, generating the inclusion of multiple types of text—from charters to lists and narratives about the institution for which they form an archive. Their commemorative function is important: "a cartulary might preserve and transmit texts for future generations," argues Joanna Tucker in a study that proscribes the genre or form of cartularies in its focus on two case studies.[3] Tucker's close assessment, which effectively opens up the field to new modes of investigation, demonstrates that a cartulary might be understood as "not just a text but...an activity," though one could introduce at this point, the mixed genre of so many Gospelbooks, which also act as cartularies in their function of gathering legal documents through time.[4]

An active cartulary is London, British Library, Additional MS 15350—the *Codex Wintoniensis* or Winchester Cartulary, an extensive volume compiled at Winchester Cathedral (Old Minster) initially in 1130–1150, with subsequent additions made later in the twelfth century at Hyde Abbey.[5]

2 Da Rold, Kato, Swan, and Treharne, *The Production and Use of English*. Ker's *Catalogue of Manuscripts containing Anglo-Saxon* influenced our decision to omit non-literary materials. Having read Ker's extensive preparatory notes and draft typescripts (Oxford, Bodleian Library, MS 20150), I think Ker may have originally intended to include charters and cartularies, too.

3 Tucker, *Reading and Shaping Medieval Cartularies*, 20. Tucker provides at pp. 8–13 a succinct history of efforts to typologize cartularies, concluding that the category is too broad to define easily.

4 Tucker, *Reading and Shaping Medieval Cartularies*, 228. Here, the most obvious examples are the Bodmin Gospels; the Old English Gospels in Cambridge, University Library, MS Ii. 1. 22; the Llandeilo/St. Chad Gospels at Lichfield Cathedral; and the Hereford Cathedral Gospels. I discuss all of these in Treharne, *Perceptions of Medieval Manuscripts*.

5 Rumble, "The Structure and Reliability of the *Codex Wintoniensis*"; England, "The

It contains the *Letter of Eadwine*—the focus of this chapter. The *Letter of Eadwine* is also included as an addition to a non-cartulary manuscript, London, British Library, Stowe MS 944—the New Minster *Liber Vitae*, the original core of which dates to ca. 1030.[6] The *Liber Vitae*, with its illustration of Cnut and Emma donating a golden cross to the New Minster in the early 1030s, famously contains the Will of Alfred, the Resting Places of Saints, many names of benefactors to the New Minster—later Hyde Abbey—and other texts, like the *Letter of Eadwine*.[7] Both manuscripts, the one a cartulary and the other a curated anthology, serve a commemorative function among their other uses, with the ongoing medieval function of Stowe 944 being principally as a Book of Remembrance.

Intrinsic evidence indicates that the *Letter of Eadwine* at it now exists was written in English in the twelfth century, perhaps specifically for its inclusion in Stowe 944, the earlier of the two extant texts. It was inserted on a blank folio—fol. 40r–v—between a list of the kings of Wessex from Ine to Cnut and a grant by William I to Riwallon, the abbot of New Minster (Fig. 1). *The Letter* fits precisely onto the recto-verso with one line to spare, and it recounts a first-person narration of Eadwine the monk's experiences in Winchester in, what is probably meant to be, the 1020s or 1030s. This earlier eleventh-century context of origin chronologically references the period of the *Liber Vitae*'s compilation in the 1030s in what then becomes a self-authentication of the manuscript as a whole. In the *Codex Wintoniensis*, meanwhile, the *Letter* is written out at fols. 116v–117r. The *Letter's* beginning is tucked up against the witness list of another diploma at fol. 116v (without the decorated and enlarged initial here that usually introduces a new instrumental text), which is datable in this context to the mid twelfth century (Fig. 2).

This possibly spurious diploma composed in Latin and in Old English refers to King Cnut's renewal of liberties to Old Minster, Winchester, in 1035.[8]

Codex Wintoniensis in its Twelfth-Century Context." *Charters of the New Minster, Winchester*, ed. Miller, 164–67, #34. Miller comments at 165 that the *Letter* is "clearly a later forgery, probably from the end of the twelfth century; probably real traditions underlie." The codex is fully digitized at the British Library's digitised manuscript website.

6 The *Letter* is generally labelled a "Writ," and is otherwise labelled as Sawyer Charter 1428, http://www.esawyer.org.uk/charter/1428.html (*Electronic Sawyer* 1428), where this version in Stowe 944 is dated "s.xii," that is, twelfth century.

7 *The Liber Vitae of the New Minster*, ed. Keynes.

8 Sawyer 976: https://esawyer.lib.cam.ac.uk/charter/976.html.

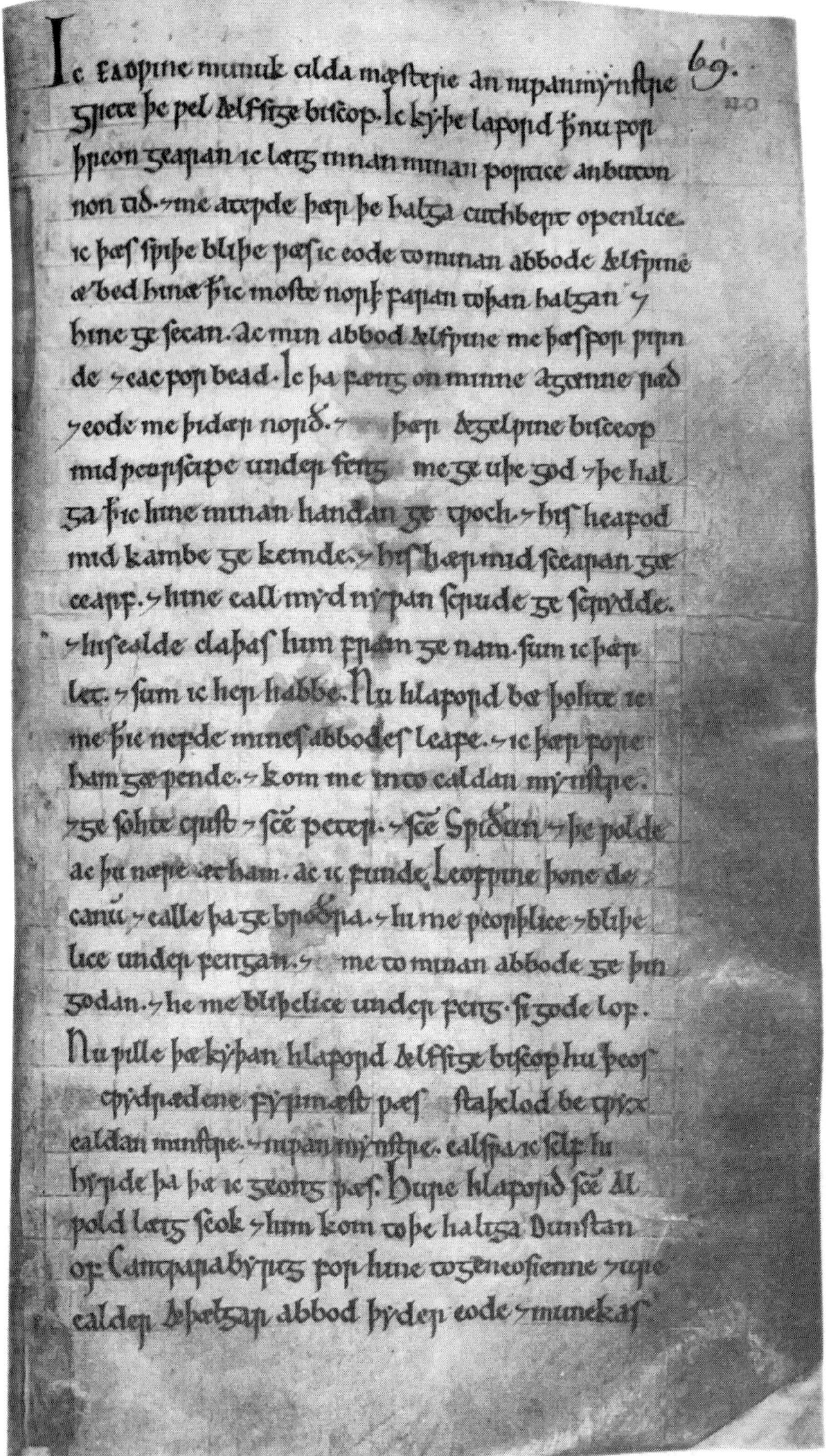

Ic Eadwine munuk ealda mæstere an niwan mynstre 69.
wrete þe wel Ælfsige biscop. Ic kyþe lauord þ nu wor
þreon gearan ic læig innan minan worlice anbutton
non tid. ⁊ me ætywde þær þe halga cuthbert openlice.
ic wæs swiþe bliþe wes ic eode to minan abbode Ælfwine
⁊ bed hine þ ic moste norþ faran to þan halgan ⁊
hine gesecan. ac min abbod Ælfwine me wæs forwyrn
de ⁊ eac forbead. Ic þa færing on minne agenne ræd
⁊ eode me þidær norð. ⁊ þær Ægelwine biscop
mid weorscipe underfeng me. geuþe god ⁊ þe hal
ga þ ic hine innan handan getoch. ⁊ his heafod
mid kambe gekemde. ⁊ his hær mid sceaan ge
ceærf. ⁊ hine eall myd niwan scrude gescrydde.
⁊ his ealde claþas sum fram genam. sum ic wær
let. ⁊ sum ic her habbe. Nu hlaword beo wolte ic
me þ ic nerde mines abbodes leafe. ⁊ ic wær fore
ham gewende. ⁊ kom me into ealdan mynstre.
⁊ gesohte crist ⁊ sce petrer. ⁊ sce Swiðun ⁊ he wolde
ac þu nære æt ham. ac ic funde Leofwine þone de
canū ⁊ ealle þa gebroðra. ⁊ hi me weorþlice ⁊ bliþe
lice underfengan. ⁊ me to minan abbode gewun
godan. ⁊ he me bliþelice underfeng. si gode lof.
Nu wille we kyþan hlaword Ælfsige biscop hu þeos
cyrcwærdene fyrmæst wes staþelod betwix
ealdan minstre ⁊ niwan mynstre. ealswa ic self hi
hyrde þa þa ic geong wæs. Hure hlaword sce Al
wold læig seok ⁊ him kom to þe halga Dunstan
of Cantwarabyrig for hine to geneosienne ⁊ ure
ealder Æþelgar abbod wyder eode ⁊ munekas

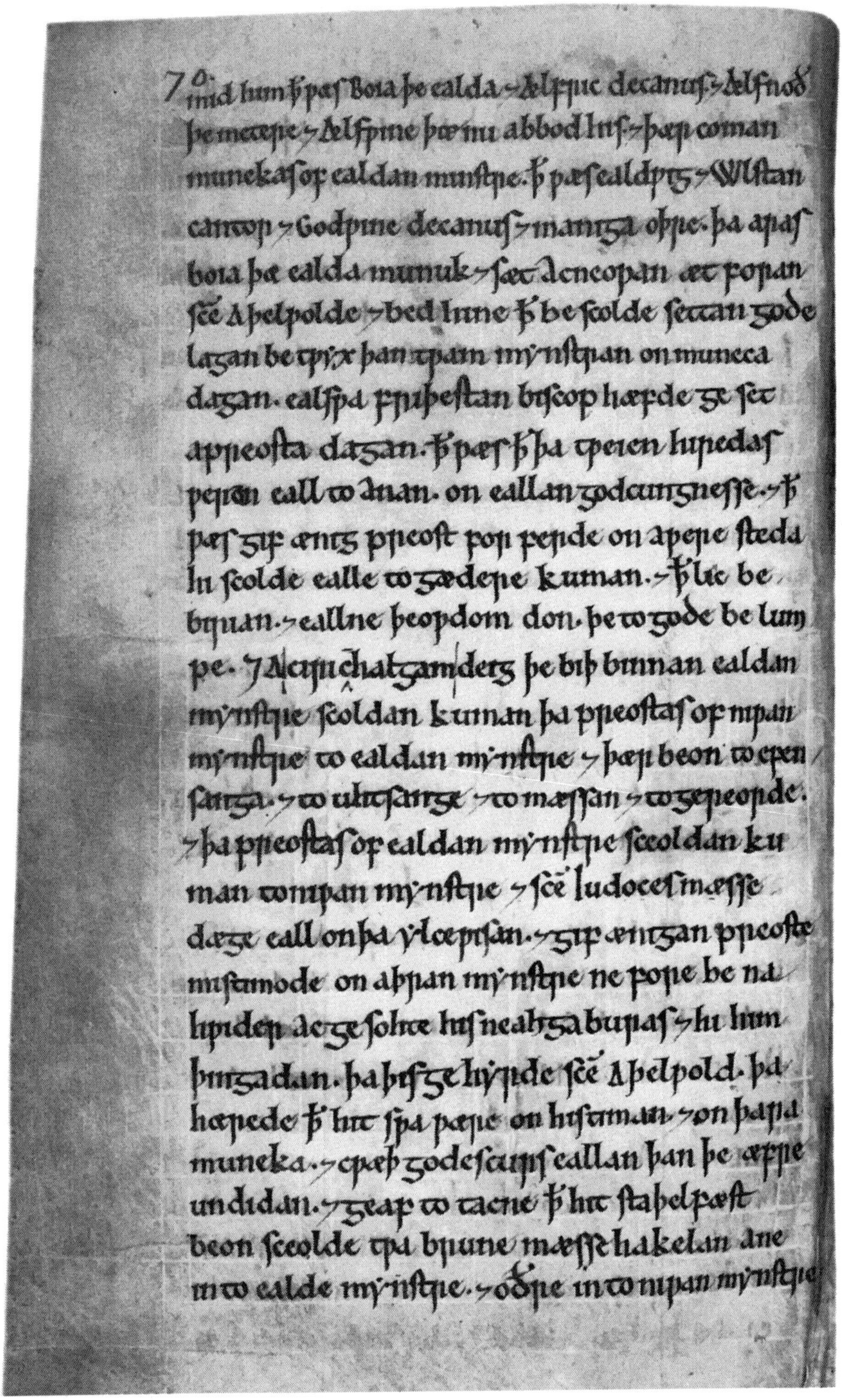
7 mid him þæt wæs Bosa þe ealda. 7 Ælfric decanus. 7 Ælfnoð
þe metere 7 Ælfwine þe is nu abbod his. 7 þær wæron
munekas of ealdan mynstre. þæt wæs ealdwig. 7 Wulstan
cantor 7 Godwine decanus. 7 manega oðre. þa aras
bosa þe ealda munuk. 7 sæt ancneowan æt wofan
sce Aþelwolde 7 bed hine þæt he scolde settan gode
lagan betwyx þan twam mynstran on muneca
dagan. ealswa Friþestan biscop hæfde ge set
on preosta dagan. þæt wæs þæt þa twegen hyredas
weron eall to anan. on eallan godcundnesse. 7 þæt
wæs gif ænig preost forþ ferde on aþere steda
hi scolde ealle to gædere kuman. 7 þæt lic be
byrian. 7 eallne þeowdom don. þe to gode be him
we. 7 ælce geare æt gangdæge þe biþ binnan ealdan
mynstre scoldan kuman þa preostas of niwan
mynstre to ealdan mynstre 7 þær beon to æfen
sanga. 7 to uhtsange 7 to mæssan 7 to gereorde.
7 þa preostas of ealdan mynstre sceoldan ku
man to niwan mynstre 7 sce ludoces mæsse
dæge eall on þa ylce wisan. 7 gif ænigan preoste
misfarode on aþran mynstre ne wore he na
hwider ac ge sohte his neahgabuwas 7 hi him
þingadan. þa þis ge hyrde sce Aþelwold. þa
hæfede þæt hit swa wære on his timan 7 on þara
muneka. 7 cwæþ godes cursas eallan þan þe æfre
undidan. 7 geaf to tacne þæt hit staþelfæst
beon sceolde twa brune mæsse hakelan ane
in to ealde mynstre. 7 oðre in to niwan mynstre

Figure 1. London, British Library, Stowe MS 944, fol. 40r–v. Images reproduced from Simon Keynes, ed., *The Liber Vitae of the New Minster and Hyde Abbey Winchester*, Early English Manuscripts in Facsimile 26 (Copenhagen: Rosenkilde and Bagger, 1996).

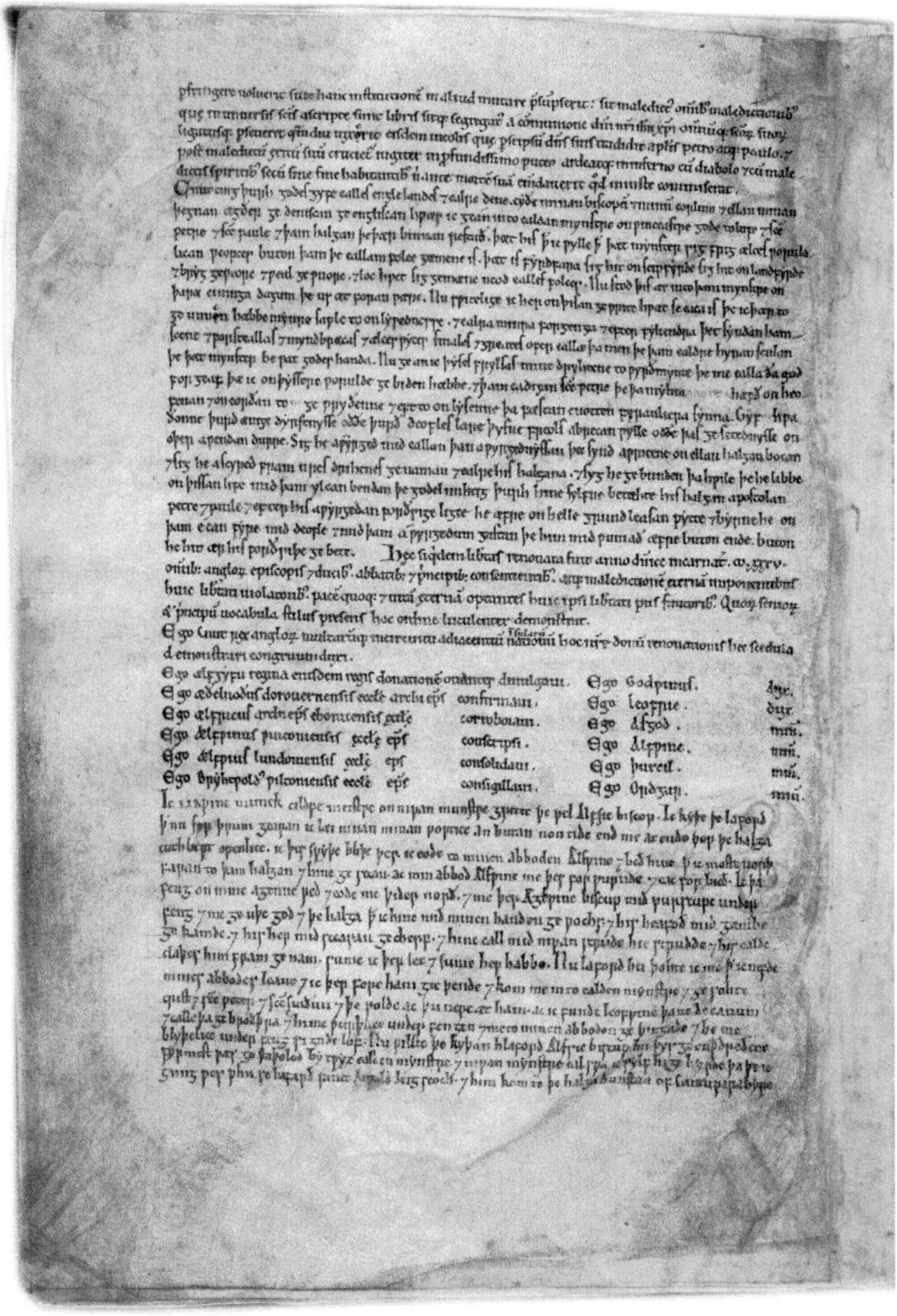

Figure 2. London, British Library, Additional MS 15350, fol. 116v.
Courtesy of The British Library Board.

Its witness list on fol. 116v anaphorically parallels the "Ic Eadwine munek cildre meistre" that introduces the *Letter* immediately below:

Ego Cnut rex Anglorum multarumque…
Ego Ælfgifu regina eiusdem regis donationem ovanter divulgari
Ego Æðelnoðus Dorovernensis ecclesiæ archiepiscopus confirmavi
Ego Ælfricus Archiepiscopus eboracensis æcclesiæ corroboravi
Ego Ælfwinus Wintoniensis æcclesiæ episcopus conscripsi
Ego Ælfwius Lundoniensis æcclesiæ episcopus consolidavi
Ego Bryhtwoldus Wiltoniensis ecclesie episcopus consigillavi
Ic Eadwine munek cildre meistre on Niwan Munstre grette…

I, Cnut, king of the English and others…
I, Ælfgifu, queen of the same king, pleased to widely share the gift
I, Æðelnoð, archbishop of the church of Dover, have confirmed
I, Ælfric, archbishop of the church of York, have corroborated
I, Ælfwine, bishop of the church of Winchester, have written
I, Ælfwig, bishop of the church of London, have confirmed
I, Bryhtwold, bishop of the church of Wilton, have confirmed
I, Eadwine, monk and child-master in New Minster, greet…

The visual integration effected by the absence of space between these texts indirectly provides further authorization to the *Letter* both formulaically and in the parallel positioning of time and place: Winchester in the 1030s. The *Letter* continues onto fol. 117r, where it is (in)completed by a curious omission of the final words that name the New Minster (Hyde Abbey).

This, then, is Eadwine's story—a "strange narrative," as Thorpe perceptively says.[9] Internal evidence naming historically attested figures (Ælfsige and Ælfwine) allows us to date the apparent events described below in the text from the Stowe 944 manuscript to 1031 or 1032.

The *Letter of Eadwine* in Stowe MS 944 (Original Text)

Ic Eadwine munuk cilda mæstere an Niwanmynstre grete þe wel, Ælfsige biscop. Ic kyþe, laford, þæt nu for þreon gearan ic læig innan minan portice anbuton nontid, ⁊ me atewde þær þe halga Cuthbert openlice. Ic þæs swiþe bliþe wæs ic eode to minan abbode Ælfwine, æ bed hinæ þæt ic moste norþ faran to þan halgan ⁊ hine gesecan. Ac min abbod Ælfwine me þæs forwirnde

9 As Thorpe in *Diplomatarium Anglicum Aevi Saxonici*, 1:321. The *Letter* from the *Codex Wintoniensis* is edited below. The editions are my own from the manuscripts and include modernized punctuation and capitalization; silent expansion of abbreviations, except here for the Tironian *nota* denoting "ond" or "and"; and the replacement of ƿ, wyn, with <w>.

⁊ eac forbead. Ic þa fæng on minne agænne ræd ⁊ eode me þidær norð, ⁊ þær Ægelwine bisceop mid we[o]rscipe underfeng me geuþe God ⁊ þe halga þæt ic hine minan handan getwoch, ⁊ his heafod mid kambe gekemde, ⁊ his hær mid scearan gæcearf, ⁊ hine eall myd nywan scrude gescrydde, ⁊ his ealde claþas him fram genam. Sum ic þær let, ⁊ sum ic her habbe.

Nu, hlaford, bæþohte ic me þæt ic nefde mines abbodes leafe, ⁊ ic þaerfore ham gæwende, ⁊ kom me into ealdan mynstre, ⁊ gesohte Crist ⁊ Sancte Peter ⁊ Sancte Swiðun ⁊ þe wolde ac þu nære æt ham, ac ic funde Leofwine þone decanum ⁊ ealle þa gebroðra, ⁊ hi me weorþlice ⁊ bliþelice underfengan, ⁊ me to minan abbode ge þingodan, ⁊ he me bliþelice underfeng: si Gode lof.

Nu wille þæ kyþan, hlaford Ælfsige biscop, hu þeos cwydrædene fyrmæst wæs staþelod betwẏx ealdan minstre ⁊ niwan mynstre, ealswa ic self hi hyrde þa þæ ic geong wæs: hure hlaford sancte Alwold læig seok ⁊ him kom to þe haliga Dunstan of Cantwarabyrig for hine to geneosienne ⁊ ure ealder Æþælgar abbod þyder eode ⁊ munekas [40v] mid him: þæt wæs Boia þe ealda ⁊ Ælfric decanus, ⁊ Ælfnoð þe metere ⁊ Ælfwine þæ nu abbod his. ⁊ þær coman munekas of ealdan minstre: þæt wæs Ealdwig ⁊ Wlstan cantor ⁊ Godwine decanus ⁊ maniga oþre; þa aras Boia þæ ealda munuk ⁊ sæt acneowan ætforan sancte Aþelwolde ⁊ bed hine þæt he scolde settan Gode lagan betwẏx þan twam mẏnstran on muneca dagan, ealswa Friþestan biscop hæfde geset apreosta dagan, þæt waes þæt þa tweien hiredas weran eall to anan on eallan godcungnesse, ⁊ þæt waes gif ænig preost forferde on aþere steda hi scolde ealle togædere kuman, ⁊ þæt lic bebirian, ⁊ eallne þeowdom don, þe to gode belumpe. ⁊ a cirichalgamdeig[10] þe biþ binnan ealdan mynstre scoldan kuman þa preostas of niwan mynstre to ealdan mynstre ⁊ þær beon to efensanga ⁊ to uhtsange ⁊ to mæssan ⁊ to gereorde. ⁊ þa preostas of ealdan mynstre sceoldan kuman to niwan mynstre ⁊ sancte Iudoces mæssedæge eall on þa ẏlce wisan. ⁊ gif ænigan preoste mistimode on aþran mynstre ne fore he nahwider ac gesohte his neahgaburas ⁊ hi him þingadan þa þis gehẏrde sancte Aþelwold, þa hærede þæt hit swa wære on his timan ⁊ on þara muneka, ⁊ cwæþ Godes curs eallan þan þe æfre undidan. ⁊ geaf to tacne þæt hit staþelfæst beon sceolde twa brune mæssehakelan[11] ane into ealde mẏnstre, ⁊ oðre into niwan mẏnstre

10 A *hapax legomenon*: "day of the consecration of the church" (See the *Dictionary of Old English*, s.v. "cyrichālgung-dæg").

11 Pfaff, *The Liturgy in Medieval England*, 511: "three copes" (?*mæssehakelan*)"—from the inventory in York, Minster Library, Additional MS 1, the York Gospels. See Ker, *Catalogue*, item 402.

The *Letter of Eadwine* in Stowe MS 944 (Translation)

I, Eadwine, a monk and childmaster in the New Minster, greet you well, Bishop Ælfsige.[12] I make it known to you, lord, that now three years ago I lay in my cell about midday,[13] and there the holy Cuthbert clearly appeared to me. At this I was very happy: I went in to my abbot, Ælfwine,[14] and beseeched him that I might go north to the saint and find him; but Ælfwine my abbot refused me and also forbade me from doing this. I then made my own decision, and went north that way, and Bishop Ægelwine received me honourably;[15] and God and the saint granted me that I washed him with my hands, and combed his head with a comb, and sheared his hair with shears,[16] and completely clothed him with new clothing, and took from him his old clothes; some I left there, and some I have here. Now, lord, I considered that I had not had my abbot's leave, and I therefore turned towards home, and came to the Old Minster, and sought Christ, and St. Peter, and St. Swithin, and would have sought you, but you were not at home; instead, I found Leofwine the dean, and all the brothers, and they received me kindly, and interceded for me with my abbot, and he received me joyfully, praise be to God!

I will now make known to you, lord Bishop Ælfsie, how this agreement was first established between the Old Minster and the New Minster, as I myself heard it when I was young, how the lord St. Ælwold[17] lay sick, and St. Dunstan came to him from Canterbury to visit him, and the elder abbot Æthelgar went there, and the monks with him: that was Boia the Old, and Ælfric the dean, and Ælfnoth the illuminator,[18] and Ælfwine who is now abbot. And monks

---

12 Bishop Ælfsige II of Winchester, who was consecrated in 1012 or 1013 and died in 1032. He was succeeded by Bishop Ælfwine (who is named in the witness list of the preceding Cnut diploma).

13 The "little hour" of sext, around noon, when monks should pray and rest.

14 Ælfwine of Winchester, who became abbot in 1031 and died in about 1057.

15 Ægelwine was bishop of Durham from 1056–1072. This figure does not match the Winchester timeline established by the bishop and abbot there.

16 See Wright, "Review: The Relics of St. Cuthbert," who mentions Alfred Westou, the keeper of the shrine of St. Cuthbert in the early eleventh century. Reginald of Durham, writing in the twelfth century, said Alfred "attained to such a degree of cordiality with the saint that it was his custom to cut the overgrowing hair of his venerable head...and to cut the nails of his fingers" (142). As Thorpe points out, at Durham, "On opening the coffin in the year 1104, there were found an ivory comb and scissors of silver."

17 Ælwold is Æthelwold, the canonised reformist bishop of Winchester from 963–984.

18 I have translated the Old English "metere" (painter) as "illuminator" here. In Worcester Cathedral Library, MS F. 34—the Tremulous Hand's version of Ælfric's

came there from the Old Minster: that was Ealdwig, and Wulfstan the cantor, and Godwine the dean, and many others with them. Boia the old monk knelt before St. Æthelwold, and prayed him that he would set good laws between the two monasteries in the days of monasticism, as Bishop Frithestan had done in the days of priests:[19] that was that the two fraternities should be all as one in all holiness: and it happened then that if any priest died in either place, they should come together and bury the body, and perform all the services which pertain to God. And on the church-hallowing day, which is in the Old Minster, the priests should come from the New Minster to the Old Minster, and stay until evensong there, and for mass, and at the mealtime. And the priests of the Old Minster should come to the New Minster on St. Judoc's mass-day entirely in the same manner. And if any priest conducted himself poorly in either monastery, he went nowhere, but he sought his neighbours,[20] and they mediated for him. When St. Æthelwold heard this,[21] he then advised that it should now be so in his time and in the days of monasticism; and pronounced God's curse on all those who should ever repeal this; and he gave, as a token that it should be so established, two dark-coloured chasubles,[22] one to the Old Minster, and the other to the New Minster.

The distinctive contexts of production, but particularly, perhaps, the inclusion of the piece in the *Codex Wintoniensis*, has led to scholars designating the text's genre as "charter," "memorandum," and "writ."[23] This description places the *Letter* firmly in the category of legal document and suggests its *notional* origin was as a single-leaf textual object. The categorization of the text as a legal object has resulted in Eadwine's story being deemed as "an obviously fake writ" and "a later forgery."[24] If those evaluating the two Eadwine texts in their manuscripts' contexts do so by the measure of the

Glossary, written ca. 1220, at 541, line 9, "pictor" is also glossed by "metere." See the *Middle English Dictionary*.

19 Frithestan was bishop of Winchester, 909–931.

20 See Saltzman, "Writing Friendship," 264. On other confraternity agreements, see Treharne, *Living through Conquest*, 114–15.

21 And thus this becomes (as Saltzman, "Writing Friendship," 65) an episcopally authorized agreement.

22 Chasuble, as opposed to cope, because a "hakelan" is an outer garment, and the outermost garment for the mass priest would be the chasuble.

23 *Anglo-Saxon Writs*, ed. Harmer, 61, seems to place the *Letter of Eadwine* under "Conventions and Formulas of Anglo-Saxon Royal Writs."

24 Miller, *Charters*, xxxvi, xxxvii, xlvi, and 165 respectively.

diplomatic, the *Letter* is a "spurious" charter, set in "fictional" periods[25]—a "fabrication," as Florence Harmer puts it.[26] In Alexander Rumble's assessment: "Although perhaps containing some elements of fact, this document as it stands is a forgery, probably fabricated in the period ca. 1170–1200."[27]

The overwhelming judgement of forgery, fakeness, fabrication, fiction, and inauthenticity indicates two notable things: the *Letter* is of value as testimony to history if, and only if, it is authentic;[28] its form and function in the world is unclear if it is not what it purports to be. Mateusz Fafinski comments that:

> Forgeries first and foremost show us how their authors wanted their past to be perceived. We tend to think about forging charters as a static event–in reality it was a process in which the past was processed for the needs of the present. Our perceptions of what constitutes a robust written record were not always the perceptions of early medieval scribes. What was paramount was the control over the memory of the past.[29]

As Fafinski suggests, for medieval scribes, there was a great deal of flexibility in the production of texts. Closed-off labelling of the short narrative in these studies, then, forecloses detailed discussion: writ, charter, memorandum proscribe the potential of the more expansive reading that the narrative seems to me to demand. Neil Ker, a more literary analyst, calls the text "The Vision of Eadwine" in his *Catalogue of Manuscripts containing Anglo-Saxon*—a roomy designation but not one that accurately reflects most of the text.[30] The short work could also be classified as "hagiographic" with its characteristics of wonder and revelation, saintly subject and posthumous miracle, and legend recast as spectacle. With this function, the scribe-authors' motivations for composing and including the texts in their specific twelfth-century contexts would be less about the Winchester minsters' historical record and diplomatic authenticity and more about a focus

25 Miller, *Charters*, 167.

26 *Anglo-Saxon Writs*, ed. Harmer, 395.

27 Rumble, "The Structure and Reliability of the *Codex Wintoniensis*," 2:346, also referencing *Anglo-Saxon Writs*, ed. Harmer, 93–95.

28 Unless, of course, the scholar is specifically focused on forgery as a phenomenon, for which see, *inter alia*, Roach, *Forgery and Memory*.

29 Fafinski, *Roman Infrastructure*, 51.

30 Ker, *Catalogue*, no. 274, item f, 338–340. At 339, "The vision of the monk Eadwine...added on a blank leaf in s. xii." At 340, "Art. f is in an angular hand of s. xii, using caroline **a**, **d**, and insular **f**, **g**, **r** and long **s**." On Stowe 944, see also Briggs, "Religion, Society, and Politics," 1:84.

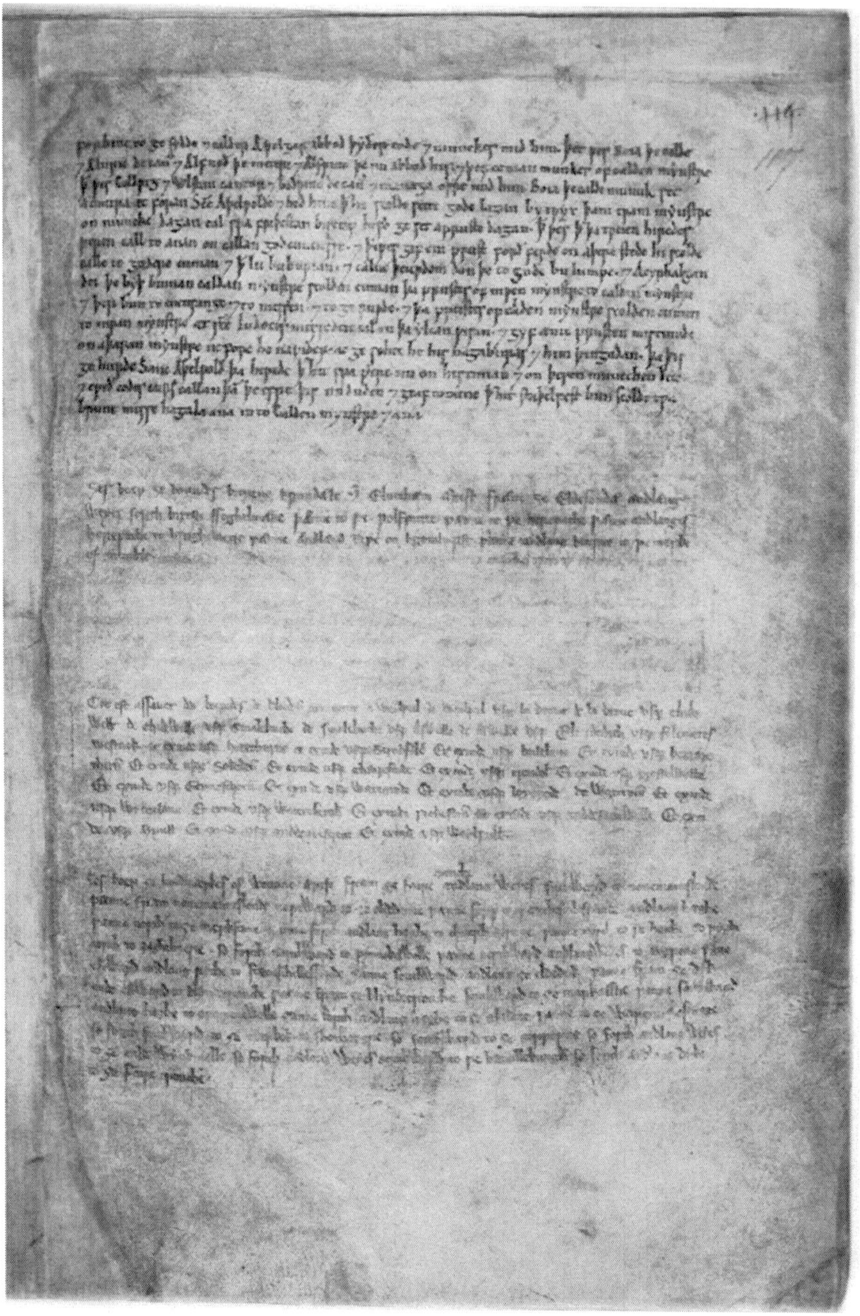

Figure 3. London, British Library, Additional MS 15350, fol. 117r. Courtesy of The British Library Board.

on institution-building and the fostering of religious connections and collective memory.

The first-person narrative creates eyewitness testimony revealing interactions and conversations between the protagonist, Eadwine, a monk and teacher of children (and thus a trusted, authoritative figure) at New Minster (later Hyde Abbey) and venerated figures associated with Benedictine institutions in the north and south of England. In her extensive commentary and edition of this text in Stowe 944, which she includes as the final item in *Anglo-Saxon Writs*, Florence Harmer comments on the rareness of the first-person address among her corpus. Only *Eadwine* and a writ issued by Cnut in the 1030s begin with the formula of "I, subject, greet." As such, it can be considered, in substance, a letter; that is, the epistolary framework of the writ justifies its consideration as simply a *letter*. This letter speaks to addressees not just in a past imaginary historical context, but also—from the distance of some 130 years and more—a twelfth-century contemporary audience in Hyde Abbey, to which New Minster was relocated in 1110 (Fig. 3).

Date and Textual History

Sean Miller, in his *Charters of New Minster* dates the recording of Eadwine's *Letter* in Stowe 944 to the second-half of the twelfth century, and the version in the *Codex Wintoniensis* to the end of the twelfth century.[31] Simon Keynes also dates the Stowe *Letter* to the second-half of the twelfth century, but inexplicably dates the *Codex Wintoniensis* to ca. 1300.[32] For Harmer, in *Anglo-Saxon Writs*, it is late twelfth century; and it is simply "twelfth century" according to Neil Ker.[33] The date of the Stowe 944 *Letter* matters in establishing the relative chronology of the two instantiations; it also matters in trying to pinpoint potential motivations for the copying of the text into these two foundational Winchester manuscripts.

Harmer's main goal in her lengthy discussion of the *Eadwine* text is to test the historical authenticity of the "writ" or "letter." She believes that the two versions were copied independently in the later twelfth century from an earlier twelfth-century exemplar, influenced by Reginald of Durham's *Libellus de Admirandus Beati Cuthberti Miraculis*—an important "little book" of

31 *Charters of the New Minster, Winchester*, ed. Miller. At 165, Miller comments the *Letter* is "clearly a later forgery, probably from the end of the twelfth century. Probably real traditions underlie."

32 Keynes, *Diplomas of King Æthelred*, 143n209.

33 *Anglo-Saxon Writs*, ed. Harmer, 388; Ker, *Catalogue*, 399.

posthumous miracles attributed to St. Cuthbert.[34] Harmer's focus on authenticating the text finds her seeking evidence for the text's copying in ca. 1170–1200 within the context of "communities...asserting their own rights as against the abbot."[35] And yes, the *Letter of Eadwine* would have resonated in a period of contentiousness between abbot and monks and it shares elements of confraternity agreements.[36] On palaeographical grounds, too, a date of post-1170 may be just right for the version of the *Letter* in Stowe 944: it *may* be; the issue of dating is complicated by a scribe who seems to be trying to make the script look earlier than it really is—the phenomenon of archaising script.

Palaeographically, the Stowe 944 *Eadwine* text can best be dated as third quarter of the twelfth century, and perhaps a little later than that dating. Precision is hard to achieve in script analysis, but specific changes in Latin and English writing at the middle point of the twelfth century were definitively catalogued by Neil Ker in his 1960 *English Manuscripts in the Century after the Conquest*,[37] and discussed with specific reference to English vernacular manuscripts by me some years ago.[38] It is likely on the grounds of features of the hand that the *Eadwine* text in Stowe 944 predates the version in the Old Minster Cartulary.[39]

The hand of the Stowe 944 *Letter of Eadwine* is curious; its features include the increasing angularity of the hand and the hybridity of key letterforms: the Caroline form of **a**, for example, together with a single compartment **a** with a slight vertical stroke on the right; two forms of **d**—both the round-backed form but with a high ascender, and straight-backed **d** which is low and squat; one form of **f** stands on the line, but there is also the typi-

34 *Anglo-Saxon Writs*, ed. Harmer, 390n2 and 391n2. Reginald's work may postdate 1172.

35 *Anglo-Saxon Writs*, ed. Harmer, 394.

36 Confraternity agreements as a genre predate 1170 by more than a century. On pre-Conquest monastic confraternities, see Saltzman, "Writing Friendship," where, interestingly for the *Letter of Eadwine,* the two houses involved in establishing confraternity are Sherborne and New Minster Winchester in the earlier part of the eleventh century (ca. 1023–1031)—the period in which the *Letter* is ostensibly placed.

37 Ker, *English Manuscripts.*

38 Treharne, *The Old English Life of St. Nicholas*; Treharne, "Production and Script of Manuscripts," 16–40; and Treharne, "Dates and Origins."

39 Comparative manuscripts include Cambridge, Corpus Christi College, MSS 303 and 367; Cambridge, Trinity College, MS R. 17. 1 (the Eadwine Psalter); and Cotton MS Vespasian D. xiv, among others. In E-Sawyer, Stowe 944 is dated to the twelfth century (http://www.esawyer.org.uk/charter/1428.html).

cal vernacular minuscule **f**; five-shaped **g** with a tail that is only sometimes closed with a hairline stroke; both Caroline and vernacular minuscule forms of **h** are present. There is frequent use of **k**; one instance of rustic **M** as a minuscule graph; long and high **s** are used, and the shoulder of long **s** has a slightly flattened top stroke. The thin and angled Tironian *nota* often sits on the line, and it has a thick downstroke at a sharp angle, just below the ruled line (which is scored). The **st** ligature is formed with long **s**; there is an example of **eth** on the last line. Curved-limbed, dotted **y** appears with very short descender, making it look more like a slightly elongated **v**. Punctuation is denoted by *punctus*; and there is one use of word-division markers at "cyriceanhaligedaige."

As a direct comparandum, the Sherborne Cartulary, dated to ca. 1170, has features I have just noted of the round and straight-backed **d**, and the long and high **s** are visible; but characteristics associated with a post-mid twelfth-century script—the 8-shaped **g**, and **t** with an onset stroke and the piercing of the headstroke by the shaft—are not visible in Stowe 944, which may then be a little earlier than 1170. One can also compare mid-twelfth-century writing by the main scribe of the *Codex Wintoniensis*, dating from ca. 1130 to 1150, and the Peterborough scribes at work ca. 1150,[40] with other English examples from manuscripts digitized by the British Library's team, such as London, British Library, Cotton MS Vespasian D. xiv (Christ Church, Canterbury, ca. 1150) and Cotton MS Julius A. ii (Canterbury(?), ca. 1150).[41]

The Stowe 944 *Letter of Eadwine* was added to a blank leaf of the manuscript, one that was scored into a *mise-en-page* of four narrow columns for, presumably, the inclusion of the names of people who entered into confraternity with New Minster. Many folios in the manuscript are given over to this commemoration of individuals.[42] Within Stowe 944 itself, the *Letter* has

40 Notable parallel hands include the main scribe of London, Society of Antiquaries, MS 60 (fols. 6–71), who is the scribe of corrections in Cambridge, Corpus Christi College, MS 134, and the second scribe of Oxford, Bodleian Library, MS Laud Misc. 636—the *Peterborough Chronicle.*

41 All Old English manuscripts in the British Library are digitized thanks to the Polonsky Foundation. They are available through the British Library website: https://www.bl.uk/ <not accessible from October 2023 to the present [July 2024]>.

42 It is interesting to note as an aside that in Stowe 944, at fol. 34r, the ages of the Virgin Mary are given in a short text that is also copied in London, British Library, Cotton MS Titus D. xxvii at fol. 56v, *and* that occurs in the hand of the later early thirteenth-century scribe in Oxford, Bodleian Library, Bodley MS 343, fol. 154v, following Ælfric's Second Series *Catholic Homily* for the Second Sunday after Epiphany: "Sancta Maria hio wæs...feowortyne geara eald þa hio Crist acende." See further Chapters 3 and 4.

specific codicological and institutional relevance, since it refers precisely to members of the New Minster community who—as Harmer and Keynes point out—are not only entered into the obits of the original core of the manuscript, some folios back, but whose names are highlighted by the addition of marginal *notae*. These annotations authenticate the names included in the *Letter* and underscore the significance of their inclusion connecting past and present in what might be an entirely fabricated story, or a narrative that is based on a New Minster/Hyde Abbey legend. Whether this fabrication *mattered* to the contemporary and succeeding audiences of the *Codex Wintoniensis* and Stowe 944 is worth considering. It was clearly an important story for the monastic community, part of an effort to present the past as still such an intimate part of the current moment.[43]

In the case of *Codex Wintoniensis*, the *Letter* was added onto the blank space of a folio late in the manuscript, immediately following a 1035 diploma of Cnut that includes two witnesses called Ælfwine (for which, see figure 2 above).[44] It may be just a coincidence that the events of the *Letter* are directly connected institutionally to the contiguous diploma. Indeed, the addition of this text is a kind of sleight of hand: its ordinariness in context; its obvious narrative expansion of Old and New Minster interests. How the *Letter* is understatedly incorporated within the *mise-en-page* is fascinating: as noted, it is a virtual continuation of the previous diploma, for, unlike many preceding folios where new texts are denoted by elaborate *litterae notabiliores*, the *Letter* is added without introduction, drawing to itself no attention.

The script of this scribe of the *Codex Wintoniensis Letter* is described by Alexander Rumble and dated by him to the second half of the twelfth century.[45] Here, the script can confidently be dated as Rumble suggests and might be, then, just a little later than the date of copying of the Stowe 944 *Letter*. Emphasizing the dates of copying of the two *Letters*, and proof of their contemporaneity of composition, are the linguistic forms found consistently through both texts. In this, the *Letter of Eadwine*—as with its script—is representative of many English manuscript productions in the twelfth century. These works demonstrate a living version of English, even as this English is clearly testifying to a distant pre-Conquest past. Both *Letters* seem to have been copied independently from what Harmer believes is a single exem-

43 As Merleau-Ponty reminds contemporary readers, in his world of embodied consciousness, the past is always embedded in the present. See *Phenomenology of Perception*, 92–102.

44 Rumble, *Winchester*, 2:222: his item 231.

45 Rumble, "The Structure and Reliability of the *Codex Wintoniensis*," 2:222.

plar.[46] Alex Rumble suggests that the scribe-editor of the Winchester version practised self-dictation in his creation of the text—reading it aloud, presumably, from an exemplar. This intriguing account of the text's production would not mitigate against Stowe 944's version itself forming the exemplar, since the two *Letters* are almost identical in substance.

Given the date of these two pieces, it is perhaps not surprising that the linguistic forms illustrate the systematic transformation of modernized Old English with the levelling of inflections, and orthographical and phonological variation seen elsewhere in texts either copied from earlier exemplars or produced contemporaneously, like Ralph D'Escures's Marian Assumption homily (for which see Chapter 2 in this volume) or the *Elucidarium* extracts in London, British Library, Cotton MS Vespasian D. xiv.[47] Both scribes of the *Letter* evince forms typical of this phase in the development of English, but so sustainedly that it seems most likely to have been a twelfth-century composition, perhaps based on earlier stories. In the opening lines, the dominance of southwest Midlands forms—<eo> to <u>, for example—in the *Codex* scribe's work testify to the superimposition of their own dialectal preferences; words like "meistre" and "sanct" in this piece suggest the explicit influence of French; <ch> for <c>, <k> for <c> in "gewochs," "kamde," and "gechearf," and other orthographical variants, indicate advanced transitional development into Early Middle English.[48] Rare vocabulary, such as "cyrichālgung" ("church-consecration") and "mistimode" ("misbehaved"), links the *Letter of Eadwine* to a handful of other late Old English texts, such as the post-Conquest manuscripts of the *Anglo-Saxon Chronicle*, or the London, British Library, Cotton MS Tiberius A. iii version of the *Regularis Concordia*.[49]

46 Harmer judged the version of the *Letter* in Stowe 944 to be contemporary with that in the *Codex Wintoniensis*. Neither, she said, could be shown to be a copy of the other. Indications that both were copied are the few corrections in Stowe 944: 40v/10: "weran" from "weron" (overwritten); line 7, **m** correct to **n** before "twam" (erased). In the later version, as Rumble points out (Rumble, "The Structure and Reliability of the *Codex Wintoniensis*," 2:346), the scribe confused long **r** with wyn at one point. Rumble suggests the cartulary scribe-editor had greater difficulty with the English than his colleague in the *Liber Vitae*. Difficulty might have arisen from the script, though, rather than the language.

47 See Younge, "The Canterbury Anthology."

48 The graph <i> indicates complete vocalization of OE palatalized /g/ in final position in "læi" (line 2, *Codex Wintoniensis*); velar fricative Middle English /χ/ < Old English /g/ is represented by <h> in *boh*.

49 "Mistimian," for example, only otherwise occurs in Ælfric's *Admonitio ad filium spiritualem*. It was taken into Middle English as "mistime."

Real, Fake: The Early Short Story

The lexical parallels with English regulations of the pre-Conquest church are hardly surprising given the nature of this *Letter of Eadwine*, which highlights and promotes central figures of the English church generally—like St. Cuthbert—but also those of the Benedictine Reform movement at Winchester and Canterbury specifically—such as Æthelwold, Dunstan, and Wulfstan the Cantor. But the conglomeration of abbots, bishops, and monks in Winchester and Durham, who could not have all been historically present in the narrative simultaneously, compromises the historical precision of the *Letter*.

The focus on the authenticity of the *Letter* as "writ" or "charter" that has constituted historians' commentaries up to this point insists on the text's productiveness being anchored principally to its specific moments of imagined production—the early 1030s, as historical figures would attest. From this perspective, it can be nothing but "spurious." However, to my mind, this is a short work—visionary, hagiographic—that transcends temporality and genre. It is a deliberate reconceptualization of received history with an eye on its present-ness; that is to say, its use for its own time of reception in ca. 1170 and subsequently. Its atemporality means it can be reused and recast for new audiences. In the second half of the twelfth century, the text can be read as a reflection of mainstream cultural trends of rising interest in institutional archival management, in property, in pilgrimage and the promotion of major cults, and, especially, in the rehabilitation of *English* saints and their relics. So it is that the definitive methodology applied to the "historical" mode of understanding—true/false, fact/fiction, authentic/spurious—really cannot account for the existence of texts like the *Letter of Eadwine*.[50] A more capacious *Eadwine* becomes indicative of an intentional social consciousness, the construction of cultural memory deliberately preserved in the books most likely to have the potential to exist in perpetuity.

Patrick Geary asks how medieval writers "reformed their pasts for their present." He comments:

> Not only did their [medieval writers'] recollections seem to contradict the image that modern historians have reconstructed of their relationship to the past, but they seemed to suppress or transform evidence that they themselves had available. This inability or disinclination to make the same sense of the past that one would today seemed far from random. Rather, it seemed part of a way of creating a present within a broadly political process

---

50 As Geary explains, building on the work of Pierre Nora and Maurice Halbwachs, in Geary, *Phantoms of Remembrance*, 10–12.

in which the nature of that present, and thus of the past which created it, was in contention."[51]

The *Letter of Eadwine*, despite the spatial, temporal, historical, linguistic, and cultural distances from an Anglo-Scandinavian Winchester, represents a determined effort to create an English narrative that reconfirms a network of belonging and community in the later twelfth-century city and its environs; this may have been a past in contention with the present, as Geary suggests, and Harmer had indicated. It provides continuity and a verification of an extended monastic family, an explicit moment of shared heritage, between the Benedictine Reform, the glory of a removed New Minster, a rebuilt Hyde Abbey, and its connections to Old Minster.

If, as seems possible, both *Letters* are roughly contemporary, situated in the later decades of the twelfth century, their moment of production might coincide with the desire to restore an equilibrium to the pasts of both the Old Minster—now Winchester Cathedral—and New Minster, now Hyde Abbey, following decades of tumult and conflict. Henry of Blois, the bishop of Winchester had had his soldiers set fire to Hyde Abbey in 1141 during the civil war between Stephen and Matilda. This had caused sustained bad feeling between the cathedral and the damaged abbey. In the early 1180s, Hyde Abbey had begun a process of politically and intellectually conscious reconstruction, developed in a thoughtful and holistic fashion in the long abbacy of John Suthill, who sought to raise funds for the Abbey's rebuilding by promoting a cult of St. Barnabas. As the story goes, in the 1180s (a decade before the miraculous discovery of King Arthur at Glastonbury) there were several sightings of St. Barnabas in the grounds of Hyde Abbey, where there was already an altar devoted to him. The cult of the saint grew significantly at this point, bringing in pilgrims and income. The twelfth century had seen the translation in Winchester Cathedral of Sts. Athelwold (1111), and Birinus, Swithun, Edda, Birstan, and Elfege in the 1150s. Hyde Abbey, without

51 Geary, *Phantoms of Remembrance*, 7. He goes on: "The right to speak the past also implied control over that which gave access to the past—the 'relics' by which the past continued to live into the present. How these tangible written relics of the past were preserved, who preserved them, and who could therefore make them to disappear were thus fundamental aspects of power and authority. The creation of the past, then, whether individual or collective, seemed far from a natural and spontaneous development from 'collective memory' or the inevitable result of the transition from 'oral' to 'literate' modes of recalling." Simon Keynes notes: "The interest in Anglo-Saxon Charters lies in the value of the documents themselves as evidence for the period in which they were produced (whether genuine or forged) and in the study of the use that has been made of them, for historical and other purposes, from the Anglo-Saxon period to present day." See Keynes, "Anglo-Saxon Charters Lost and Found," 49.

seeming to engage in one-upmanship, had its own saints and collection of relics to promote. Barnabus led the way; Cuthbert, by Eadwine's account, was already present in the abbey through his clothing at the very least.[52]

These events of the *Letter of Eadwine* are particularly pertinent—even if it is, as historians point out, a "forgery"—for the "openlice" (public) appearance of a saint, Cuthbert, which very much echoes the appearance of Barnabus. Within the *Letter*, the illusion of temporal accuracy is provided in the sequence of the narrative through the precision of detail; Eadwine recounts the conversation he had with his abbot and relives the welcome he received from the monks at Old Minster when he sought their assistance on his return from Durham. The text reconceives of the past in an impossible way—fictionalising (through this first-person, named, and eyewitnessed account) a heyday of obedience and forgiveness, of collegiality and unity: a glorification, but also a reflection upon, and promotion of, a past that is validated not only by its temporal appropriateness with the physical book-context itself in the case of Stowe 944, but also its self-authentication in the names of characters in the *Letter* being listed in the original *Liber Vitae*. This work, then, like other English texts copied in the twelfth century among earlier texts, is confirmed by its specific context; the inclusion, in Stowe 944, within a whole group of pre-Conquest textual items authorizes and validates the cuckoo in the nest.

Indeed, the *Letter of Eadwine* is not trying to be real or fake any more than other literary texts like hagiography or romance might be; its cultural valence is not the distant, pre-Conquest one. It is the contemporary. Representing the monastic obligation to remember, to venerate, and to eulogize, in order to fill in the textual gaps, the audience has to supply knowledge or social consciousness that the text itself does not provide. The testifying to the historical truth of the text's own self comes from the act of writing of this part-hagiography, part-history, part-institutional, self-aggrandising into the cartulary. Its inclusion there emphasizes its central role in Winchester's promotion. This knowledge is chiefly about the devotion by Winchester monks to saints like Cuthbert (long revered by Anglo-Saxon kings from Athelstan to Cnut[53]), and, of course, to Æthelwold.

---

52 This interpretation, of the communal gathering in of Cuthbert as a saint to whom monks at Hyde could be devoted, counters the interpretation of Cuthbert's cult offered by Whitehead, *The Afterlife of St. Cuthbert*, which sees Cuthbert as being promoted at this time as principally local, regional in impact. Whitehead does not seem to know the *Eadwine* texts.

53 Rollason, "St. Cuthbert and Wessex: the Evidence of CCCC MS 183," 413–24, discusses the "interest taken by the kings of the West Saxon house and later by the Danish Cnut, in St. Cuthbert and his community" (413).

Devotion in Action

We should applaud the skill of the *Letter*'s author in creating a literary pastiche with key moments dependent on a broader intertextuality contained within the host manuscripts themselves. When Eadwine disobeys his abbot and takes his own advice to seek Cuthbert's relics—he who has divinely intervened in Eadwine's life—he engages in an otherwise chronicled episode, described by Symeon of Durham in his twelfth-century account of Durham and its principal saint, *Libellus de Exordio*.[54] In Symeon, we learn of Alfred Westou, great-grandfather of Ælred of Rievaulx, who tended the incorrupt body of St. Cuthbert in the 1020s, and collected relics of other Northumbrian saints. Here we learn that:

> Temporibus antiquis quidam Elfredus Westove exstitit qui admiranda dilectionis gratia apud beatum Cuthbertum speciali prerogativa effulsit. Nam seram ipsius sepulcri aperire ei licenter et impune licuit, quociens ei libuit, circa eum quae voluit componere, et quae desiderabat ab eo citius impetrare praevaluit. Unde traditur eum tantae dulcedinis gratia apud ipsum ex familiaritatis noticia succrevisse quod nonnunquam ipsius venerandi capitis comam supereffluentem soleret tondendo praecidere, capillos pectine Eburneo dividendo et deliniendo emollire, digitorum ungues pulcritudine rotundata excidere.
>
> In days of old there flourished one Elfred Westove, who, for the love which he bore to St. Cuthbert, was distinguished by peculiar privileges conceded to no one but himself—for, as often as it pleased him, he might freely and with impunity open the coffin of the Saint, *might wrap in such robes as he thought fit*—and he could obtain from him, without delay, whatever he requested: when it is recorded that he, from long familiarity, attained to such a degree of cordiality with the Saint, that it was his custom to cut the overgrowing hair of his venerable head, to adjust it by dividing it and smoothing it with an ivory comb, and to cut the nails of his fingers, tastefully reducing them to roundness.[55]

---

54 Rollason, *Symeon of Durham*, 161–62.

55 *Symeon of Durham*, 161–62. This story was further embellished by Reginald of Durham, for which see *Reginaldi Monachi Dunelmensis*. On the vestments at Durham, see Cuthbert's Maniple (https://trc-leiden.nl/trc-needles/individual-textiles-and-textile-types/religious-vestments-and-other-textiles/st-cuthbert-embroideries). The two garments were probably presented to St. Cuthbert's shrine, then at Chester-le-Street just north of Durham, when King Æthelstan, son of Edward the Elder and stepson of Ælflaed, whose capital was at Winchester, paid a visit to the shrine in 934 and donated several garments, including a stole with a maniple.

Eadwine appropriates the role of corporeal carer for himself in the twelfth-century *Letter*, and in so doing, creates a tight bond between Winchester's religious establishments and Durham. This link is reinforced in Stowe 944 by the twelfth-century inclusion, as Florence Harmer notes, too,[56] of relics of St. Cuthbert, listed by Hyde Abbey: "De barba Sancti Cuthberti et de vestimento eius" ([Relics] of the hair of St. Cuthbert and of his clothing"), as if to back-up the narrative.[57]

In the light of the increase in the movement of relics in the twelfth century, and the active development of major saints' cults, this text and its claims becomes a promotional exercise, exclaiming Cuthbert's presence at Hyde Abbey and the Old Minster. The subsequent inclusion of significant Old and New Minster saints—Judoc and Æthelwold (though Æthelwold was not formally canonized)—augments the utility of the *Letter* and enhances the reputation of the city's institutions. This text, then, can be read within the broader twelfth-century context of the revival or re-instigation of Early English saints' cults, like those of St. Neot and St. Chad. Elsewhere, I have suggested that these two saints' lives in London, British Library, Cotton MS Vespasian D. xiv, and Oxford, Bodleian Library, Hatton MS 116, respectively, rather than being assigned to the pre-Conquest period, should be assigned to a post-Conquest date of origin or adaptation in their current, unique forms.[58] Similarly, we might see in this brief narrative of Eadwine an attempt in the twelfth century to raise the profile of major English saints in the (then) here and now.

Such promotion of native saints would be especially important in the light of the diminution of Æthelwold and others' status after the Norman

56 *Anglo-Saxon Writs*, ed. Harmer, 389.

57 See *Anglo-Saxon Writs*, ed. Harmer, 391. Cuthbert's hair has long been a source of miraculous powers; St. Cuthbert's relics were dispersed early: "Bede records one of his hairs being used for a miraculous cure in the eighth century," as commented on by Bailey, "St. Cuthbert's Relics", 236. On medieval hair, see https://www.livescience.com/54644–mysterious-braided-hair-medieval-saint.html describing the hair of a saint found at Romsey. Bartlett discusses the significance of the first haircut, for which there were liturgical directions, even (see https://dutchanglosaxonist.com/2015/10/22/splitting-anglo-saxon-hairs-cuthberts-comb/). Incidentally, one might also note the work of Borges in *La cifra*, "El hombre ha muerto. / La barba no lo sabe. / Crecen las uñas." ("A man lies dead; / yet his nails, beard and hair / continue to grow, unaware.") Note, that Ælred of Rievaulx, Elfred Westou's great-grandson, became an authority on St. Cuthbert; see Meehan, "A Reconsideration," 255. On the biblical significance of hair, see Matthew 10:30 ("Even the number of hairs on your head are numbered"), Luke 1:18, and Chapter 3, below.

58 See Treharne, *Living Through Conquest*.

Conquest. Walkelin, bishop of Winchester, ignored the cult of Æthelwold, for example, since *he* favoured Swithun, particularly because Swithun was a canon-bishop, not a monk-bishop.[59] Æthelwold's cult was honoured, though, by Bishop William Giffard, successor to Walkelin. He translated, as mentioned, the relics of the saint in 1111; and then all of Winchester's main saintly relics were translated in 1158 by Henry of Blois. In fact, this precise moment of the translation of saints might have been inspirational to the scribe-editor of the *Letter of Eadwine*, hopeful of promoting Winchester once again as a major site of pilgrimage.[60]

In this short but fascinating text—an addition to two well-known manuscripts that have been only partially explicated—layers of production and reception, of composition and retelling, are revealed. Eadwine retells his own story and highlights a notable, if fictitious or reconstructed, event involving a significant episcopal agreement that emphasizes the roles of English monks in establishing community and belonging that is centuries old. This partially-hagiographic narrative is retold in the monumental memorial manuscript, Stowe 944; and then retold again—in a specifically archival and *documentary* context in the *Codex Wintoniensis*.

Such retelling and recontextualization highlights the story of English in the twelfth century, especially through later additions to manuscripts that are often overlooked or separated from their physical contexts. These additions highlight the timelessness of manuscripts; the manuscript's ability to remain inhabited, living, throughout the centuries. The posthumous incorruptibility of St. Cuthbert and the efficacy of the holy corpse emphasize, too, the significance of the salvific text, thought to live meritoriously within the permanent book into a sure eternity.

Finally, within their twelfth-century contexts, specifically as thoughtful and integrated additions to pre-existing English codices, the *Letter of Eadwine* and other works, like the English poem, *The Grave (discussed in detail in Chapter 3)*, are linked in their intentionality and functionality. As Eadwine celebrates English saints, so *The Grave* in Oxford, Bodleian Library, Bodley MS 343, a manuscript of ca. 1170–1200, celebrates St. Wulfstan, among other English saints and authors. Both texts are about corporeality: the life, death, and survival of the subject saint, curiously told partly through the survival of

---

59 See Browett, "The Fate of Anglo-Saxon Saints." See also Browett, "Touching the Holy."

60 As Browett, "Touching the Holy," shows, contact relics were very much on the rise in the eleventh and twelfth centuries. From this short story, both the comb and the vestments of Cuthbert would have been attractive to pilgrims, useful for the promotion of the cathedral, and, by its association with its own set of vestments, Hyde Abbey.

hair as a whisper of humanity continuing beyond the existence of the body. More, the *Letter of Eadwine* highlights the surviving corporate identity of the body politic in the shape of Winchester's ecclesiastical institutions and their inherited social consciousness. It is this emphasis that motivates the *Eadwine* scribe-authors, reminding us in our present—essentially—of the longevity of pre-Conquest memories, and of Old English, beyond the political, historical, cultural, and generic delimitation imposed by contemporary scholarly categories. To read this text, then as so much more than a spurious writ or fake charter is to give back to it a life and reality it clearly had in the second-half of the twelfth century for Winchester monks. It has humorous moments, a clear-sighted sense of its own importance for its place of production, and so much to tell present-day readers about the imagination and sense of community of its author(s) and institutions. To resist pigeonholing, to allow the short text to tell its own story, is to reveal many possibilities of interpretation each of which resists easy answers and offers instead multiple avenues for future research.

Codex Wintoniensis,[61] *Letter of Eadwine*, fols. 116v/line 35–117r

Ic Eadwine munek cild[r]e meistre on niwanmunstre grette þe wel, Ælfsie biscop. Ic kyþe þe, laford, þæt nu for þrum gearan ic læi innan minan portice anbutan nontide, end me ateude þer þe halga Cuthbert openlice. Ic þes swyþe bliþe wes ic eode to minen abboden Ælfwine, 7 bed hine þæt ic moste norþ faran to þam halgan 7 hine gesecan. Ac min abbod Ælfwine me þes forwurnde 7 eac forbie[d]. Ic þa feng on mine agenne red 7 eode me þider norð, 7 me þer Æge'l'wine biscup mid wurscupe underfeng 7 me geuþe God 7 þe halga þæt ic hine minen handen gewochs, 7 his heafod mid gambe gekamde, 7 his her mid scearan gecherf, 7 hine eall mid niwan scrude his scrudde, 7 his ealde claþes him fram genam. Sume ic þer let, 7 sum ic her habbe.

Nu, laford, buþohte ic me þæt ic nefde mines abbodes leaue, 7 ic þerfore ham gæwende, 7 kom me into ealden mynstre, 7 gesohte Crist 7 Sancte Peter 7 Sancte Suiðun 7 þe wolde ac þu nere æt ham, ac ic funde Leofwine þane decanum 7 ealle þa gebroðþra, 7 hi me wurþlice underfengen, 7 me to minen abboden geþingade, 7 he me blyþelice underfeng: si Gode lof.

Nu wille þe kyþan, hlaford Ælfsie biscup, hu þys gecuþdreðene fyrmest wæs gestaþolod betwyx ealden mynstre 7 niwan mynstre, ealswa ic sylf hi

61 Since each text of the *Letter* is a unique attestation to this short story, I provide here a conservative edition of the *Letter* as it appears in the *Codex Wintoniensis* for comparison with the version provided above from Stowe 944.

gehyrde þa þe ic gung wes: whu se lafard sanct Alwold leig seoch. 7 him kom to þe halga Dunstan of Cantuwarabyre [fol. 117r] for hine to gesydde 7 ealdor Æþælgar abbod þyðer eode 7 munekes mid him: þet wes Boia þe ealda 7 Æluric decanus, 7 Ælfnoð þe metere 7 Ælfwine þe nu abbod his. 7 þer coman munkes of ealden mynstre: þæt wes Ealdwig 7 Wlstan cantor 7 Godwine decanus 7 managa oþre mid him; Boia þe ealde munuk set acneuwa ætforan Sancte Aþelwolde 7 bed hine þæt he scolde sette Gode lagan betwyx þam twam mynstre on muneke dagan, ealswa Friþestan biscup hefd geset apruste dagan, þæt wes þæt þa tweien hiredes weren eall to anan on eallan godcunnesse, 7 þæt wes gif eni prust forðferde on aþere stede hi scolde ealle togædere cuman, 7 þæt lic buburian, 7 ealne þeuwdom don, þe to gode bulumpe. 7 a cyrhalgandei þe byþ binnan ealdan mynstre scolden cuman þa prustes of niwen mynstre to ealden mynstre 7 þær bun to euensange 7 to messen 7 to gerurde. 7 þa prustes of ea'l'den mynstre sceolden cumen to niwan mynstre æt sancte Iudoces messedeie eal on þa ylcan wisan. 7 gyf ænie prusten mistumde on aþaran mynstre ne fore he nawider ac gesohte he his nagaburas 7 him þingadan. þa þis gehurde Sanc Aþelwold, þa herede þæt hit swa were nu on his timan 7 on þeren munechen deie, 7 cweð [g]odes curs eallan þan þe efre undudan. 7 geaf to tacne þæt hit staþelfest bun scolde twa brune messehagala ana into Ealden mynstre, 7 ana [into niwen mynstre].

Chapter 2

KNOWN AND UNKNOWN

AUTHORS AND TRANSLATORS

THIS CHAPTER WILL examine a text from London, British Library, Cotton MS Vespasian D. xiv, using it as a test-case for how scholars understand anonymity and authorship, originality and dependency, and translation and adaptation in this period. It is common to privilege literature of known authors; to privilege original texts, rather than later instantiations; and texts that are faithfully rendered through translation rather than adaptation. The homily by Ralph D'Escures for the Virgin Mary was a contemporary text for the compiler of Vespasian D. xiv in his mid-twelfth-century Christ Church manuscript and was included in a newly made English translation.[1] It is edited in full at the end of this chapter, and it clearly unsettles the categories of literary production that are most favoured in the modern academy by being simultaneously ordinary yet startling; new but old; and dependent yet thoroughly different by virtue of its specific manuscript context and physical manifestation. Its audiences may have been varied, too; certainly, the manuscript made its way from Christ Church Canterbury into female ownership later in the twelfth century.

Original versus Copy

Each version of a medieval text, whether it was originally composed in the late tenth century or composed in English following an English exemplar in the late eleventh century, or composed as a translation from Latin into English in the twelfth, is a witness to a deliberate creative act specific to its own place and time. Numerous representations of anonymous sermons or homilies of the late Old English writer Wulfstan I, Archbishop of York, and the monastic author Ælfric are incorporated into post-Conquest manuscripts, and usually shown only through the critical apparatus at the foot of the page of scholarly editions. In this presentation, these texts are fragmented into variants—selected spelling differences or lexical differences in the later texts as compared with earlier versions of that text. Yet, in manu-

1 This chapter is a major expansion and revision of parts of Treharne, "The Life of English in the Mid-Twelfth Century."

script transmission, there is no such thing as a "copy"—no two manifestations of a handwritten text are the *same*. Each, then, deserves its own modern account tracing individual decisions made by the manuscript compilers, the scribes, and subsequent annotators, whether those decisions appear conscious or, in the case of scribal idiolectal idiosyncrasies, unconscious.[2]

As well as multiple representations of sermons or saints' lives, there are also texts in twelfth-century manuscripts that sit uneasily within modern categorizations: they are "original" literary works, despite being explicitly religious and formulaic; they are original in the sense that they contain lexis, orthography, or syntax that is peculiar to them, despite being explicitly transferred from an earlier manuscript context into a later one (usually regarded as just "later copies"); they are original in their target language (English in this case) despite being translated from Latin, or perhaps French; in their inclusion in manuscript anthologies containing texts dating from ca. 990 into the twelfth century, they are neither Old English nor Middle English, sitting comfortably alongside one another; and they are original, because they will be read and interpreted differently according to the perspectives of new audiences through time. London, British Library, Cotton MS Vespasian D. xiv—as a whole volume—reflects many of these trends in English literary production in this period. Compiled in the mid-twelfth century at the Benedictine cathedral of Christ Church, Canterbury, this extensive volume contains two Latin prayers, and fifty-two English texts, including homilies written by Ælfric; a unique *Life of St. Neot*; a version of the *Dicts of Cato*; and two twelfth-century translations—excerpts from the *Elucidarium* by the monastic writer Honorius *Augustodunensis*, and a homily on the Virgin Mary by Ralph D'Escures.[3]

These two definitively post-Conquest translations are interesting as witnesses to the very latest compositions in "Old" English, or, as some scholars would have it, the very earliest in "Middle" English.[4] Hahn, for example, has stated of the *Elucidarium* and the Marian homily that:

---

2 On the act of "copying," see Scase, *Visible English*, Chapter 5.

3 The English homily on the Assumption of the Virgin Mary is edited and translated in full at the end of this chapter. Readers who are unfamiliar with the homily might start with that, and then come back to the discussion that follows here. Cotton MS Vespasian D. xiv is digitized at the British Library digital manuscripts website. All the texts are edited by Warner, *Early English Homilies*. For the contents and description, see Ker, *Catalogue*, item 209; and Wilcox, *Wulfstan Texts*, 53–64. The most recent scholarship on this manuscript is significant for the manuscript's history and use; see Treharne, *Living Through Conquest*; and Younge, "Canterbury Anthology."

4 Cited in Laing's *Catalogue of Sources*, at 83, is Clark's comment from *The Peterborough Chronicle* that the Ralph D'Escures piece is "usually classed as the earliest M[iddle] E[nglish]." See Hahn, "Early Middle English," 61–91.

> These renderings of near-contemporary Latin texts stand among the first specimens of e[arly] M[iddle] E[nglish], and, like the heterogeneous character of the *Anthology* [Vespasian D. xiv] as a whole, document how the native tongue had begun to negotiate various domains of cultural production.[5]

The "native tongue" had, of course, been negotiating "domains of cultural production" by the twelfth century. The linguistic demarcation of texts in the twelfth century (or even the later eleventh) from "Old" into "Middle" English has no basis beyond the scholarly legacy of labelling and categorizing, which was done in the nineteenth and twentieth centuries on philological grounds and, it must be said, for pragmatic disciplinary and pedagogic purposes. It is precisely because of the categories of period and language history that twelfth-century English had been overlooked until the late 1990s and early twenty-first century. For the compiler(s) of Cotton Vespasian D. xiv there seems to be *no* recoverable distinction between the way in which the language of the texts was regarded: some of the texts are relatively closely transmitted from pre-Conquest exemplars, while many use later forms of vocabulary, phonology, accidence, and spelling. The compiler did not distinguish between these; "Old" and "Middle" English, then, co-exist harmoniously in this manuscript, indicating that the rigid chronology scholars assign nowadays to language evolution simply has no relevance to the manuscript compilers, scribes, and anticipated audiences within the twelfth-century moment of production.

To a greater or lesser extent, then, these texts were simply the compilers' required vernacular materials, which, we must accept, were considered as equally intelligible to the intended reader-listeners. There was a distinct tolerance of linguistic variability within written texts in the post-Conquest period, very much foreshadowing the emergence of remarkably divergent dialectally marked texts in the later twelfth century and thereafter. English materials copied in the post-Conquest period, particularly those based on Old English exemplars, should not be written off simply as archaic or as a corrupt form of some linguistic *koine* previously more perfect, as indeed they often are.[6]

---

5 Hahn, "Early Middle English," 82–83. Hahn gives no evidence for naming this manuscript the *Rochester Anthology* other than the inclusion of the piece by Ralph D'Escures, who, as he points out, was bishop of Rochester (82n41). D'Escures was also archbishop of Canterbury. Moreover, as noted below, D'Escures's homily was copied into Worcester Cathedral Library, MS F. 94 in the early twelfth century, a manuscript whose origin is Worcester. In other words, there are no grounds for calling this manuscript the "Rochester" anthology.

6 Milroy, "Middle English Dialectology," 193, states: "Variability in Middle English [equally well applied to the twelfth century] has sometimes been perceived as

Environments of Production and Use

The precise environment in which these early English texts were read and used in the twelfth and thirteenth centuries is often difficult to determine.[7] It is generally thought that religious manuscripts such as Cotton Vespasian D. xiv were compiled because homiletic and hagiographic texts were "needed for religious instruction in the vernacular, to lay people as well as to nuns and monks."[8] These conclusions assume that preaching was, on occasion, performed in English, and that secular clergy were able to read and assimilate, or copy for themselves, the materials included in these manuscripts.

These theories could indeed account for the post-Conquest compilation of manuscripts containing English texts. But, often, such conjecture cannot be entirely substantiated by the meagre evidence that the manuscripts themselves provide and it is unlikely in the long post-Conquest period up to 1220 or so—that manuscript use was homogenous or audiences monolithic.[9] In addition, although the surviving homiletic and hagiographic manuscripts are often treated as a group, particularly because of the shared genres of the volumes, their intended uses may have varied depending on where and when they were produced, but also the manuscripts' later uses.[10] In practical terms, the production of manuscripts must have depended on available personnel and materials: the institution had to have at least one compiler or supervisor who recognized the need for English texts; there had to be one or more scribes capable of writing English; at least one Old English

---

an obstacle rather than a resource...In editorial and descriptive commentary, it is very easy to find comments about chaotic or 'lawless' spelling and even editorial judgements to the effect that a given scribe could not have been a native English speaker—so variable is his orthography...However, judgements of this kind can effectively block further investigation of variable constraints in the texts in question: they can be dismissed as 'corrupt' or 'unreliable' specimens of language."

7 See, for example, Irvine, "The Persistence of Old English in the Twelfth Century" and Treharne, "The Production of Manuscripts Containing English Religious Texts in the First Half of the Twelfth Century." See also Richards, *Texts and Their Traditions*.

8 Sauer, "Knowledge of Old English," 796.

9 In relation to preaching in her *Old English Homilies*, lii-liii (where she states of Bodley 343), Irvine suggests "[it] shows no sign of having played any direct role in preaching...It shows none of the omission marks, changes in punctuation, and marginal additions that appear in eleventh-century manuscripts like D and F, and which would be usual in a manuscript intended or used for preaching. Moreover the material is not uniformly suitable for preaching purposes."

10 See Treharne, "Production of Manuscripts." For analysis of the use of Vespasian D. xiv by religious women, see, most recently, Treharne, "'Miserere, meidens.'"

exemplar from which texts could be copied; and sufficient facilities to enable the production. Surviving evidence suggests that such a combination of conditions was limited to certain religious institutions, which included Durham, Ely, Peterborough, Sherborne, Winchester, and especially Rochester, Christ Church, Canterbury, and Worcester. These latter three have more than one significant or extensive vernacular manuscript attributed to them.[11]

In theory, Cotton Vespasian D. xiv could have been written for preachers as a form of homiliary or general religious miscellany; as a collection of texts for monastic students; as a compilation of works suitable for female readers; or as a volume always generally intended for private, devotional reading. It seems most likely, though, that this is a monastic production initially intended for a monastic audience.[12]

Texts are adapted and manipulated throughout the codex to eliminate references to material that is not relevant for monastic recipients, who should be understood to include a variety of audience members, not simply a uniform group of Latinate and educated men in the coenobitic order. The monastic community would be home to many differing individuals (from *conversi*, to lay brothers, to members of the confraternity, including women), whose language, intellectual talents, commitment to the order, and institutional roles would merit a diversity of textual materials for a variety of purposes.

Vespasian D. xiv is a well-produced, thoughtful, and extensive compilation that confirms the literary relevance and cultural usefulness of English in this post-Conquest period. The inclusion of the translation of Ralph D'Escures's homily on the Festival of the Virgin Mary highlights this. Ralph D'Escures—at one time abbot of Séez, then bishop of Rochester up to 1114 and archbishop of Canterbury until his death in 1122—wrote his Latin homily in ca. 1100, and, until the work of Wilmart, it was thought to be by Anselm.[13] With a pericope of Luke 10:38–42, the homily was intended by its author to be used at the Assumption of the Virgin Mary, celebrated on August 15th. It forms a cluster of five English pieces in Vespasian D. xiv that centres on Marian feast-days, and indicates that the place of origin of this codex was

11 This evidence of monastic manuscript production in English problematizes the theory that French was the spoken language of the monastery proposed by Crane in her essay, "Anglo-Norman Cultures in England, 1066–1460," 44. Short likewise comments that "Anglo-Norman was a language of law and of record, an acceptable alternative to Latin in the cloister," in "Language and Literature," 205. Neither Short nor Crane cite their sources for this use of French in the cloister.

12 See Younge, "Canterbury Anthology."

13 Kienzle, "Exegesis on Luke 10:38." Wilmart, "Les homélies attribuées à S. Anselme," 339–41.

participant in the emerging Marian *cultus* in the twelfth century, and paid especial attention to the Feast of the Assumption.[14] Included in Vespasian D. xiv are D'Escures's piece (rubricated here as *Sermo in festis Sancte Marie virginis*), three texts, or parts of texts, for the Assumption of the Virgin,[15] and an extract from Ælfric's Homily on the Annunciation from his *Catholic Homilies I*. The occurrence of these homilies in two parts of the codex, correctly sequenced—three in one grouping, the D'Escures piece some one hundred folios later, and the Annunciation of Mary appearing as the penultimate text—indicates an organizational scheme very loosely approximating to two separate, thin sequences of *temporale* and *sanctorale* pieces, interspersed with other texts.

The English version of D'Escures's text was, it seems, part of the original design of the manuscript written by the main scribe and occurring at fols. 151v–157r, following the unique *Life of St. Neot* (feast-day July 31).[16] The text is carefully measured for the twelve folios upon which it is written, beginning at the top of fol. 151v and ending precisely with a half-word runover at the foot of fol. 157r. It is introduced by a red and green large initial **S** and a rubric in red at the very top of the folio, where "Marie" is picked out by a green capital **M**. It precedes a brief, integral extract in English from the *Trinubium Annae* which begins at the top of fol. 157v (with no decoration in the opening phrase). The latter text (edited below), the earliest vernacular rendition of its source, is intimately linked with the Festival of Mary by its provision of the lineage of the Virgin, and an explanation of the various Marys of the New Testament attempting to clarify the protagonists of Luke 10:38–42, who form the main homily's focus.

The Latin homily is significant for numerous reasons, not the least of which is its manner of composition. Ralph D'Escures writes that he delivered it first in French to his chapter before transcribing it into Latin:

> Quid ad gloriosam virginem Dei Genitricem lectio ista pertineat, ut in ejus festivitate legatur, plerique solent quaerere: unde quid ego sentirem, in conventu fratrum prout potui, vulgariter iam plusquam semel exposui.[17]

---

14 On the devotion of some monastic establishments to the Virgin in this period, see Hall, "The Earliest Anglo-Latin Text," 104–37.

15 Items xvi, xvii, and xviii in Warner, *Early English Homilies*. Item xvi and xviii are two separated parts of Ælfric's *Catholic Homilies I* text on the Assumption, while the intervening item, xvii, is from Ælfric's *Catholic Homilies II* text on the Assumption.

16 Love, "St. Neot," 331, states: "The relics [of St. Neot] were inspected in the late eleventh century, and certified to be authentic by Anselm, archbishop of Canterbury." On this *Life*, see Treharne, *Living Through Conquest*.

17 Kienzle, "Exegesis on Luke 10:38," 22. My translation.

> Many people often inquire how this reading is relevant to the glorious virgin, the Mother of God, any why it is read on her feast day. Therefore, I have already explained more than once to the assembled brothers where I stand on this matter, as best I could, in the common tongue.

D'Escures's explication of the Lucan pericope provides insight into the process of homiletic composition. The "common tongue" used to discuss the Festival of the Annunciation among the monastic chapter is likely to have been French, given that D'Escures himself came from Séez, and it is from this oral delivery of a proto-sermon that the Latin text originated. Notes would presumably have been taken on tablets and used as the basis for the formal Latin. This is followed by a performative reversal when the Latin was translated into English, possibly for oral delivery to an audience of monks, novices, or, perhaps, lay brothers and *conversi*.

Allegory and Twelfth-Century Modes of Living

The English text in Vespasian D. xiv stays fairly close to its source, but it emphasizes the significance of the Virgin Mary, reflecting major theological trends in the twelfth century, as the cult of Mary grew. The source will have been a Latin text of the homily similar to that edited by Kienzle in 1997 from the early twelfth-century manuscript, Worcester Cathedral Library, MS F. 94.[18] It retains the pericope, but in English, and the vernacular version then omits D'Escures's preface outlining his dedication and exposition of how the homily came about, as well as his more general series of statements about exegesis and a particular allegorization of *castellum* with its obvious resonances for interpreting the Virgin from scriptural reference. Notably, then, the authorship of the homily is not significant to the Vespasian D. xiv compiler (or the compiler of the exemplar). The English is rendered anonymous, as was so often the case in English manuscripts. Authority comes less from the known author, and more from the written production itself.

The structure of the main body of the Old English homily follows that of the Latin source. The symbolism of Mary as the "castle" into which Christ entered, signified by Martha's house, becomes the impetus for the detailed allegorization of Mary's walls of virginity and her representation as a tower of humility.[19] This leads into a narration of the Annunciation, which is

18 Kienzle, "Exegesis on Luke 10:38." See Thompson, *Catalogue of Manuscripts of Worcester*, for a description of this manuscript, and his Plate 26 for a portion of the text.

19 This is, as Mateusz Fafinksi reminded me, reminiscent of lines 14–17 of the third of the Old English *Advent Lyrics*, a sequence of antiphons, where Jerusalem is employed to show the Virgin's unique qualities as both mother and virgin, her words "Ic eam Drihtenes þenen" ("I am the handmaid of the Lord") being used to support her humility. From this, the homilist expands the discussion: the gate of faith through which Christ entered the Virgin was not despoiled, since he is, as his name signifies, the Saviour.

The second half of the homily concerns Mary and Martha as symbols of the contemplative and active lives, respectively: two facets of life that are unified within the Virgin Mary herself. Neither Mary nor Martha could achieve the accomplishments of Christ's mother, but each in their own chosen tasks is following Christ's commands. The active life of Martha is demonstrated in the Virgin's merciful acts, an aspect of the symbolism that allows the homilist to allude to the care of the baby Jesus, the Flight to Egypt, the Massacre of the Holy Innocents, and the Crucifixion and Resurrection. In all these things was the Virgin troubled. The contemplative aspect of Mary's life in Luke 10:38–42 is enacted through the care with which the Virgin listened to Gabriel, and literally interiorized the wisdom and virtue of God. Since the Virgin, in being "lifted up over the angels" and reunited with Christ, was no longer troubled, this contemplative part represents the best part, that which shall never be taken away.

The symbolism of the roles of Martha and Mary as active and contemplative was widely commented on throughout the medieval period, by Gregory, Jerome, Bede, Augustine, Hrabanus Maurus, Ælfric,[20] Honorius *Augustodunensis*, and many other commentators. While the unification of the aspects of both of Lazarus's sisters within the singular figure of the Virgin, emerged from at least the ninth century, it does not appear to be until the later eleventh and twelfth centuries that the interpretation of Mary as unifying the active and contemplative, and choosing the latter as the best part became fully advanced.[21] Thus, not only was Ralph D'Escures's homily reflecting contemporary twelfth-century theological developments, but also the English translation in Cotton Vespasian D. xiv was a deliberate effort to ensure that innovative and current exegesis was made available in English. It is, in sum, the earliest allegorization of Mary as "cæstel" in English.

---

as Mary: "nimeð eard in þe, swa hit ær gefyrn / witgan wisfæste wordum sægdon; / cyðdon Cristes gebyrd, cwædon þe to frofre, / burga betlicast" ("Jesus makes a home in you, as it was prophesied long ago with wise prophets' words; they revealed Christ's birth, they spoke as a comfort to you, best of cities.").

20 For the cult of the Virgin Mary generally in Anglo-Saxon England, and the Feast of the Assumption particularly, see Clayton, *The Cult of the Virgin Mary*, 232–44.

21 See Constable, *Three Studies in Medieval Religious Thought*, 3–141, especially 8–10, 45. See also Baker and Kienzle, "Monastic Preaching and the Sermon."

The Old English begins with the gospel story itself in a relatively full discussion of chapters 38–42. This section closes with the point that:

> Sume ungelærede mænn wundrigeð hwæt þiss godspell belimpe to þære eadigen Marien, Cristes moder, and hwi man æt hire þenunge geræde þiss godspell; ac us þincð þæt hit rihtlice to hire gebyreð beo þan þe ure larðeawes us doð to understandene.
>
> Some unlearned people wonder what this gospel has to do with to the blessed Mary, Christ's mother, and why this gospel is read at her service; but it seems to us that it properly pertains to her just as our teacher helps us to understand.

Within this short unique passage, which comes before the translation proper from D'Escures's Latin source, the adaptor is clearly addressing not the "ungelærede mænn" at whom many modern scholars believe English texts in this period are aimed, but others—the "us"—who set themselves apart from this group and who have access to the teaching of the author (a change from the Latin first-person narrative of Ralph D'Escures). This is a theologically aware audience who would not doubt the appropriateness of Luke's passage for an exegetical interpretation of the Virgin.

After the introductory statements, the English abbreviates an exposition on the nature of the symbolic to get to the main subject matter quickly. It follows the Latin homily by relating relatively complex exegesis that links the distinctive qualities of Mary and Martha—as contemplative and active—as united characteristics centred within the Virgin's single person. The Latin source is closely followed throughout the English homily: the same structure is adhered to; and the same tropes for explaining the interpretation are present. For example, the following quotation figuratively elucidates the image of the "castellum" of Mary and Martha into which Christ entered as guest of the Virgin Mary herself:

> Ðes cæstel þære ure drihten in com betacneð rihtlice þæt synderlice unwæmme mæden Maria, Cristes moder. For cæstel is geclypod sum heh stepel þe byð mid wealle betrymed swa þæt æigðer oðre bewereð wið unwinen gewinne.
>
> Ðyssen cæstele is rihtlice wiðmeten þæt synderlice mæden Marie, Cristes moder. For heo wæs fæstlice betrymed mid mæigne unwæmmes mægeðhades on lichame and on geðanca swa swa mid strangen cæstelwealle, swa þæt hire næfre ne mihte genelæcan nan lichamlic galnysse, ne forðen to hire geðanca nan ungelefed hæmeðe. And forþanþe mægeðhad stranglice mæig wiðstanden þære galnysse þæt hit ne byð þurh þæt oferswiðen. Modignysse gelomen gewinð þa infare, forþan wæs eadmodnysse stepel on hire [and wal] þe aferseð ealle modignysse fram þan mægeðhade. And forþan þe eadmodnysse wiðstant modignysse, þæt heo ne byð þurh þæt oferswiðen galnysse gelomen gewinð þa infare, forþan wæs mægeðhades

weall on hire þe stranglice [fol. 152v] aferrsed ealle galnysse fram eadmodnyssen steple. And swa is mægeðhades weall and eadmodnysse stepel and æigðer mid oðren gestrangod þæt on hire mægeðhade næfre ne mihte gefæstnigen modignysse, ac æfre hire wæs on eadmede mægeðhad and clæne eadmodnysse.

This castle into which our lord came rightly signifies that uniquely undefiled maiden Mary, Christ's mother. For a castle is protected by a high tower which is enclosed by walls so that each protects the other against enemies in conflict.

This castle is rightly compared to that unique maiden Mary, Christ's mother. For she was securely enclosed with the might of pure virginity in body and in mind as if with strong castle walls, so that no bodily desire might ever approach her, nor any illicit act of fornication come to her mind. And therefore virginity can strongly withstand desire so that it cannot be overcome by it. Pride might frequently attack the entrance, yet humility was the tower within her and the walls of her virginity resisted all that pride. And because humility withstands pride, so that she cannot be overcome by the frequent attacks of lust at the entrance, then the wall of virginity resolutely repels all lust from the tower of humility. And so the wall of virginity and the tower of humility are each strengthened by the other such that in her virginity she might never be overcome by pride, but humble virginity and pure humility were always in her.

As the figurative "cæstel," Mary is protected by the mutually reinforcing tower of humility and the walls of virginity in body and mind such that no pride or lust can enter.[22] The translator stays close to the Latin source phrase by phrase, sense by sense, abbreviating some clauses slightly, and expanding with minor details for clarity (by, for instance, adding "Cristes moder" in the third sentence). Interestingly, the English version is linguistically conservative with a high proportion of Old English vocabulary employed. There is only one "modern" loanword: "cæstel." Much of the vocabulary is Ælfrician in nature, so that relatively rare words like "wiðmeten" ("compared"), "bearneacinde" ("pregnant"), "earplættigen" ("hit about the ears"), and "ateorigendlice" ("transitory") appear to be based on a thorough knowledge of Ælfric's prose. How this text could be considered "early Middle English" is an interesting question, then.[23]

22 This effective, visual image is significantly developed in later medieval literature including Robert Grosseteste's *Chasteau d'Amour* and its derivative, the *Cursor Mundi*, as well as shorter texts, like Thomas Hales's *Love–Ron*: "Wyþ þeoves, wiþ reveres, wiþ lechers / Þu most beo waker and snel; / Þu art swetture þane eny flur / Hwile þu witest þene kastel."

23 Contemporary twelfth-century lexemes include "estlice" ("graciously"), "herbyrge" ("lodgings"), wiðtogan ("taken away from"), and "gelichamede" ("clothed with flesh").

Translating for Clarity

Apart from the language used in this text, other aspects of the translator's techniques demonstrate a concern to achieve the greatest possible clarity in the English version. Some extraneous matter, not pertinent to the specific emphasis of this text's main interpretation, is excised; for example, the name of Elizabeth, mother of John the Baptist, is excised in the English. Elizabeth's annunciation is employed as a comparison to the Virgin's in the Latin source, whereas in the English "Hit wearð fullfremod on hire [Mary] þæt þæt se ængel hire sæde" ("It was fulfilled in her just as the Angel told her").[24] The vernacular version maintains its focus on the Virgin. The homilist here would be conscious of the genealogical clarification that comes in the *Trinubium Annae* appended to the homily, which negates the need for comparison with Elizabeth at this point, since the *Trinubium* effectively explains Mary's family tree and her relationship to her aunt, Elizabeth.

Other excisions from the Latin include the attempt to explain Mary's humility and virginity. D'Escures reminds his audience that any virgin like Mary, who was about to get married, would ponder the significance of Gabriel's statement concerning the immaculate conception:

> Si cuilibet virgini desponsatae in animo suo disponenti nubere diceretur, filium habetis, non miraretur neque interrogaret quomodo istud fieret utpote quae se desponsatam et in proximo nupturam sciret et a viro gravidari usu naturae speraret. Haec autem non immerito mirata est, et quomodo quod promittebatur fieret, sciscitata quoniam quamvis desponsatam, tamen se nunquam nupturam, neque virum cognituram certissime sciebat. Hoc de virginitate.[25]
>
> If a woman, who was promised to any man and was disposed to get married, was told, "You will have a son," she would not wonder, or ask how that might happen as she knew she was engaged and expected to get married soon, and she hoped to become pregnant by her husband according to the usual nature of things. However, she not unjustly wondered how what was promised would occur, asking because even though she was engaged, she knew for certain that she would neither marry nor have any physical knowledge of a man. This is about her virginity.

---

24 "Quia enim credidit, perfecta sunt ei a Domino quae ab angelo dicta sunt, sicut ait ad eam Elizabeth" (Kienzle, "Exegesis on Luke 10:38," 25, lines 82–83); "For because she believed, the things spoken by the angel were perfected for her by the Lord, as Elizabeth said to her."

25 Kienzle, "Exegesis on Luke 10:38," 24, lines 50–56. My translation.

The English abbreviates this to:

> Gyf ænige mædene þe hæfde gemynt were to underfone and wære gesæd þæt heo scolde sune geberen, ne þuhte hit hire sellic, ne heo axigen nolde: "Hwu sceal hit gewurðen þæt ic sune gebide?" Ac eaðe þeos mihte axigen: "Hwu sceall þiss gewurdeðen þæt ic sune habbe?" For þeh heo Josepe gehandfæst wære, þehhweðere he hæfde anrædlice on hire gemynte þæt heo næfre weres gemænnysse nolde cunnen.

> If any virgin who had a mind to be married to a man were told that she would bear a son, might it not seem strange to her, might she not ask: "How can it be that I should expect a son?" But easily might this woman [Mary] ask: "How shall this come about that I shall have a son?" For though she was engaged to Joseph, nevertheless she had resolutely resolved that she would never have intercourse with a man.

Here, the "natural order" of marriage and pregnancy is omitted in the English, keeping a close focus on the miraculousness of the Virgin's conception. The English makes more personal and emotive the normal human reaction Mary showed to Gabriel's extraordinary news. Mary's statement of intent to remain a virgin permanently is emphasized in the English through the addition of Joseph's name, amplifying the audience's understanding of the direct speech and Mary's life-long commitment to her purity.[26]

The minor addition of Joseph's name in the English version is typical of the translator's clarifying of the Latin by adding small details such as "Cristes moder" ("Christ's mother") to the Latin "Maria" to ensure the audience understands to which Mary the text refers. The Old English also insists at all points on the superlative nature of Mary's endeavours. Where, for example, the Latin discusses the way Martha and Mary's attributes are brought together uniquely in the Virgin, it states:

> Nunquam in aliqua persona, immo in omnibus, Martha sic operata est; nunquam in sic alias, Maria contemplationi vacavit. Nunquam sic alias haec vel illa quod suum est exhibuit. Cum Martham vel Mariam dico, earum significata intelligo.[27]

> Never in any one person, but rather in all, did Martha work like this; nor has anyone devoted themselves to contemplation as Mary did. Never has anyone else performed such actions or exhibited such contemplation as these two did. When I mention Martha or Mary, I am referring to what they symbolize.

---

26 It is conceivable that this insistence on Mary's continence can be regarded as an allusion to the twelfth-century conciliar canons trying to enforce clerical celibacy. See Pelikan, *The Christian Tradition*, 163–64.

27 Kienzle, "Exegesis on Luke 10:38," 25, lines 95–98.

The English adds to this description the uniqueness of the Virgin:

> On nanre oðre næs Marthe studdinge on nanen time swa fullice geforðed toweard Gode and toweard his leomen swa on ures Drihtenes moder. Ne Marien besceawunge ne hire hlystinge to Godes worden næs næfre on nanre oðre swa fullice geforðed swa on ure Drihtenes moder.
>
> In no one else was Martha's labour at any time as fully accomplished towards God and towards his body as in our Lord's mother. Nor was Mary's contemplation nor her listening to God's word ever in any way as fully accomplished as it is in our Lord's mother.

The English version augments the Latin to intensify the superlative nature of the Virgin, both in her role as the perfect embodiment of the active and contemplative, and in her role as the mother of God. This movement towards the specific identification of the Virgin as glorious perfection is very much in keeping with theological developments in the twelfth century, which strove to stress the importance of Mary as mediatrix and Virgin Mother.[28] The English version of the D'Escures homily, to a greater extent than the original, is testimony to this Mariological process.

Inextricably linked with the glorification of Mary in this period is the reminder of the humanity of the mother of God, which the English intensifies. This emphasis comes more from the incremental build-up of related expansions in the English, rather than from any explicit statement. In the enumeration of the six corporal mercies, Mary is shown in the role of young mother to the baby Christ. The Latin explains that Mary received Jesus, clothed him, fed him, quenched his thirst, looked after him during sickness, bathed him, soothed him, comforted him ("infirmum per infantiam iacentem non solum visitavit sed etia balneando, fovendo, leniendo, gestando frequentavit").

In the English version, the six mercies are directly linked to Judgement Day and the homilist reinforces the need for charity and generosity, before going on:

> Swa swa leofne gyst heo hine husede and innlice herebyregode. Ðonne he hnacod wæs, heo hine beswreah mid lichame and mid reafe. Ðonne he wæs hungrig and þurstige, heo hine estlice gefylde mid hire meolca. On his cildlicen unfernysse, heo hine baðede and beðede, and smerede and bær, and frefrede and swaðede and roccode. Swa þæt man mæig rihtlice beon hire secgen, Martha wæs bisig and cearig emb þa þenunge.

28 Pelikan, *The Growth of Medieval Theology (600–1300)*, 160–74.

> So just like a beloved guest she housed him and harboured him inwardly. When he was naked, she wrapped him with a body and clothed him. When he was hungry and thirsty, she graciously filled him with her milk. In his childhood helplessness, she bathed him and warmed him, and anointed him and carried him, and comforted him and swaddled him and rocked him. So a person may rightly say about her, Martha was busy and full of care about service to others.

The touching and detailed expansion of the mother's cares for her child allows the audience to engage with Mary, to envisage her motherly actions in a sequence of events that through their timing and intimacy would be familiar and touching. This comes immediately prior to the capture and execution of Christ—the telescoped time adding to the drama and demand for empathetic response. In the English, the sudden transition from Mary's care of her baby to her grief at Christ's crucifixion, where Christ's death "þurheode hire sawle" ("pierced her soul") is startling. Though the homily is written in the third person, the demand for affective response from the English audience is broadly reminiscent of the intimate piety of Anselm's prayers. This moment in the homily pre-empts the much more introspective devotion to the Virgin seen in later twelfth-century or earlier thirteenth-century texts, such as the *On God Ureisun of Ure Lefdi*, which is similarly inspired by the office for the Feast of the Assumption.[29]

A significant expansion in the English text concerns the definition of what constitutes the active and contemplative lives as represented by Martha and Mary, and as mentioned above. The debate was to take on added force when the contemplative life signified by Mary became associated with the monastic life as the *optima pars*. By the twelfth century, while the lives were distinguished, it was their compatibility and unification either in Mary or in Christ that dominated both artistic and textual discourse.[30]

In D'Escures's homily, he comments of Mary and Martha that:

> Duae istae sorores, sicut sancti patres plenissime nobis exposuerunt, duas in sancta ecclesia vitas designant: Martha scilicet, activam; Maria, contemplativam. Ista laborat ad exhibenda indigenti omnia humanitatis officia; illa vacat et videt quoniam Deus est.[31] Ista circa exteriora occupatur; illa interiora contemplatur.[32]

---

29 See, for example, Renevey, "Enclosed Desires," 50–52.

30 For a general discussion of these issues, see Constable, *Three Studies*, especially 44–92.

31 See Psalm 45:11.

32 Kienzle, "Exegesis on Luke 10:38," 25, lines 88–93. My translation.

> These two sisters, as the holy fathers have fully explained to us, signify two lives within the holy Church: namely Martha, the active life, and Mary, the contemplative life. The former works to fulfill all the offices of humanity towards those in need; the latter is still and sees that God is present. The former is occupied with external matters; the latter contemplates internal matters.

This interpretation of Martha and Mary—with the former working by showing all the occupations of kindness to the needy, and the latter devoting herself to stillness in the presence of God—is interestingly expanded in the English:

> Ðas twa gesustre beo þan þe ure larðeawas us cyðeð betacnigeð þa twa lif þe man lætt on rihtwisnysse: Martha þæt geswyncfulle lif þe we one drohtnigeð; Maria þæt ece lif þe we to willnigeð. Martha swanc and becarcade to geforðigene þan Hælende and his þeowen þa lichamlice behefðen; Maria fæstlice wunede abuten þan Hælende and hlyste his worden. Seo studdede emb þa uterlice þing; þeos oðer þa inweardlice þing gemyndelice besceawode.

> These two sisters about whom our teachers inform us signify the two lives which are permitted to a person in righteousness: Martha is the active life of the kind which we lead; Mary that eternal life to which we aspire. Martha laboured and was anxious to take care of the Saviour and serve his physical needs; Mary resolutely stayed around the Saviour and listened to his words. The one troubled about the outer things; the other contemplated spiritual things inwardly.

The minor alteration in the English has consequences for interpreting how the translator understood or wished to convey the meaning of the active and contemplative lives. There is no doubt that while the two figures of Mary and Martha were uniquely united in the Virgin Mary, the distinction between the two lives was very real for this writer. For Ralph D'Escures, the distinction appears to be one of pastoral and charitable activity versus a metaphorical and spiritual stillness, perhaps in the virtual *peregrinatio pro amore Dei* of the coenobitic life. Rather like the structure of the *Ancrene Wisse* and the stipulations of the author, the outer concerns, while necessary, are secondary to the inner: the physical and temporal in opposition to the spiritual and eternal.

For the English translator, D'Escures's practical distinction is adapted explicitly into one that signifies the time lived in this present manner (the active life) from the time to come (the contemplative). The variation between the Latin and the English is subtle, but notable. The English writer seems deliberately to have altered the emphasis away from the need of the *vita activa* to be busy, to a particular mode of conduct in this lifetime. It is a hint that "the kind of life we lead" might refer to the writer and audience's lives of pastoral care, or some form of activity in this lifetime. The hope for the *vita contemplativa* is necessarily the hope expressed through Mary's "best part" of being re-united with Christ in heaven: a part, which as the translator says, "us geunne God þurh hire þingunge" ("God might grant us through her ministry"). This interpretation belongs specifically to the Augustinian conception of the two lives: "What Martha did is what we are; what Mary did is what we hope for."[33] Moreover, the translator's alteration of the source to encapsulate Augustine's interpretation can be directly linked to Ælfric in his homily on the Assumption of the Virgin from his *Catholic Homilies II*, which takes Augustine's sermons as a major source.[34] It is possible that the English writer borrowed from Ælfric at this point in the text, since Ælfric's own Assumption homily appears earlier in Cotton Vespasian D. xiv, where the text reads (at fol. 55v): "On þyssen twam gesustren wæron getacnode twa lif—þiss geswyncfulle þe we onwunigeð, and þæt ece þe gewillnigeð" ("In these two sisters were symbolized two lives—this active one that we lead, and that eternal one which we desire").[35]

In addition to the adaptations already discussed, the most significant departure from the Latin source is the entire omission of the twenty-line laudatory verse to Mary, Christ, and the Trinity at the end of the homily, which takes the audience through Mary's uniqueness as virgin mother to the divinity of the son she bore. The emphasis is predominantly on Christ and his great sacrifice. The English text instead contains the addition of the *Trinubium Annae*, maintaining the focus on Mary. This latter short text appears to be integral to the D'Escures homily, only divided from the main homily by an enlarged initial **A**. This explication of the Holy Kinship narration, ultimately derived from the second-century *Proto-Evangelium* of James, adds considerably to the understanding of the homily since the respective Marys' relationships, among others, are fully explained. This appendage is the earliest vernacular rendition of the *Trinubium Annae*, the first Anglo-Latin version of which comes from Bury St. Edmunds in the late eleventh century, and used in another context altogether.[36] The provision of it as an appendix to the Ralph D'Escures homily illustrates the wholesale imaginative recontextualization of the material to an explanatory function, bearing directly on the preceding text, and situating Mary in her most human context.

---

33 Augustine, *Sermons* 103–4, cited in Constable, *Three Studies*, 18n75.

34 Godden, ed., *Ælfric's Catholic Homilies, Second Series*, Homily 29, lines 38–40, 256: "On ðisum twam geswustrum wæron getacnode twa lif. þis geswincfulle ðe we on wuniað. and þæt ece ðe we gewilniað." For the commentary and sources of this homily, see Godden, ed., *Ælfric's Catholic Homilies: Introduction*, 588–92.

35 Both homilies are written by the main scribe of Vespasian D. xiv. See Warner, *Early English Homilies*, 48–49.

36 See Hall's discussion of this text, with an edition of the English version in Cotton Vespasian D. xiv, in "The Earliest Anglo-Latin Text," 104–37.

It is the case, therefore, that while the English version of the D'Escures Assumption homily remains substantively true to its source, it seeks both to improve clarity, and to incorporate minor re-readings at various points that show both tradition in the use of Ælfrician homiletic material, rhetoric and diction, and innovation in simultaneously participating in twelfth-century religious developments in Marian devotion. The transmission of this English homily demonstrates that texts in the vernacular in the post-Conquest period were no less sophisticated, theologically informed, or learned than their Latin sources and analogues, despite a tendency on the part of modern critics to undervalue this body of twelfth-century English material. This undervaluing comes from the overemphasis on "originality"; that is, so-called "copies" are not valued, and *translations* from Latin into English are not treated as literary equals with those composed in English itself. This homily both in Latin and Old English reflects the desire of the Vespasian D. xiv compiler to offer contemporary analysis of a Lucan pericope, and to provide not simply the homilies of Ælfric for the Assumption, but something more indicative of post-Conquest devotional developments. That the compiler had no concern about melding pre-Conquest English with post-Conquest vernacular material in the same manuscript and often contiguously is testimony to the vitality of the former well beyond its usually perceived sell-by date.

This text is one of many hundreds written in Early English with a dependency on a pre-existing instantiation. It is a moving and evocative work that, once studied for its own merits, shows the potential of examining early literature in its context of production. The homily is representative of a wider trend in the compilation of manuscripts written in English that counters scholarly misconceptions about the period: from these texts we witness the educated nature of the audience despite the tendency to downgrade English to a medium fit only for the *illiterati*; we witness the dissemination of contemporary theology, despite the desire to situate English texts as testimony only to retrospectivity; we witness the institutional requirement for the production of texts and manuscripts, despite a general scholarly unwillingness to accept the potential of the English vernacular for literary expression; and we witness an adaptive creativity in twelfth-century English which parallels that preceding the Conquest, despite scholarly assumptions that much copied in English from 1060 to 1220 is backward-looking imitation.

The original Early English text of Ralph D'Escures's *Sermo in Festis Sancte Marie Virginis* and its modern English translation are set in parallel on the following pages.

Early English Version of Ralph D'Escures's *Sermo in Festis Sancte Marie Virginis*, Cotton Vespasian D. xiv, fols. 151v–158r[37]

SE GODSPELLERE LUCAS sæigð on þyssen godspelle þæt se hælend com into sumen cæstele, and sum wif hine underfeng into hire huse, þære wæs to name Martha. Seo hæfde ane suster þe wæs genæmd Maria. Seo wæs sittende æt ures drihtenes foten and hlyste his worden. Ac Martha beswanc and bestuddede þa lichamlice behefðen. Seo stod and cwæþ to þan hælende: "La drihten, nis þe na gemynde þæt min suster lætt me anen þenigen? Sæge hire þæt heo me fylste." Se hælend hire andswerede and cwæþ: "Martha, Martha, þu eart bisig and gedrefed on feale þingan. Ac anlypig þing is behefe: Maria hæfð gecoren þæt beste dæl þæt hire næfre ne byð wiðtogan."

Sume ungelærede mænn wundrigeð hwæt þiss godspell belimpe to þære eadigen Marien, Cristes moder, and hwi man æt hire þenunge geræde þiss godspell. Ac us þincð þæt hit rihtlice to hire gebyreð beo þan þe [fol. 152r] ure larðeawes us doð to understandene.

Đes cæstel þære ure drihten in com betacneð rihtlice þæt synderlice unwæmme mæden Maria, Cristes moder. For cæstel is geclypod sum heh stepel þe byð mid wealle betrymed swa þæt æigðer oðre bewereð wið unwinen gewinne. Đyssen cæstele is rihtlice wiðmeten þæt synderlice mæden Marie Cristes moder. For heo wæs fæstlice betrymed mid mæigne unwæmmes mægeðhades on lichame and on geðanca swa swa mid strangen cæstelwealle, swa þæt hire næfre ne mihte genelæcan nan lichamlic galnysse, ne forðen to hire geðanca nan ungelefed hæmeðe. And forþanþe mægeðhad stranglice mæig wiðstanden þære galnysse þæt hit ne byð þurh þæt oferswiðen. Modignysse gelomen gewinð þa infare, forþan wæs eadmodnysse stepel on hire [and wal] þe aferseð ealle modignysse fram þan mægeðhade. And forþan þe eadmodnysse wiðstant modignysse þæt heo ne byð þurh þæt oferswiðen galnysse gelomen gewinð þa infare, forþan wæs mægeðhades weall on hire þe stranglice [fol. 152v] aferrsed ealle galnysse fram eadmodnyssen steple. And swa is mægeðhades weall and eadmodnysse stepel and æigðer mid oðren gestrangod þæt on hire mægeðhade næfre ne mihte gefæstnigen modignysse, ac æfre hire wæs on eadmede mægeðhad and clæne eadmodnysse.

37 Edited by Warner, *Early English Homilies*, 134–39, item xliii. Re-edited here from manuscript, with silent expansion of abbreviations and followed by my own translation. The text is also published by Kluge, *Angelsäschisches Lesebuch*, 87–90.

Modern English Translation of Ralph D'Escures's *Sermo in Festis Sancte Marie Virginis*

THE GOSPEL-WRITER LUKE says in this gospel that the Saviour came into a certain castle and a woman, the name of whom was Martha, received him into her house. She had a sister who was called Mary. She was sitting at our lord's feet and listened to his words. But Martha worked and troubled about one's bodily needs. She stood and said to the Saviour: "Oh lord, don't you mind that my sister lets me serve alone? Tell her to help me." The lord answered her and said: "Martha, Martha, you are busy and troubled about many things. But only one thing is needed: Mary has chosen that best part which shall never be taken away from her."

Certain uneducated people wonder how this gospel pertains to the blessed Mary, Christ's mother, and why someone at her service reads this gospel. But it seems to us to be justifiably relevant to her and something our teachers help us to understand.

This castle into which our lord came rightly signifies that uniquely undefiled maiden Mary, Christ's mother. For a castle is protected by a high tower which is enclosed by walls so that each protects the other against enemies in conflict. This castle is rightly compared to that unique maiden Mary, Christ's mother. For she was securely enclosed with the might of pure virginity in body and in mind as if with strong castle walls, so that no bodily desire might ever approach her, nor any illicit act of fornication come to her mind. And so virginity can strongly withstand desire so that it cannot be overcome by it. Pride might frequently attack the entrance, yet humility was the tower within her and the walls of her virginity resisted all that pride. And because humility withstands pride so that she cannot be overcome by the frequent attacks of lust at the entrance, then the wall of virginity resolutely resisted all lust through the tower of humility. And so the wall of virginity and the tower of humility are each strengthened by the other such that in her virginity she might never be overcome by pride, but humble virginity and pure humility were always in her.

Genyme we us þæt godspell to gewitnysse hire mægeðhades and hire eadmodnysse. Ða þa se ængel hire cydde þæt heo cænnen scolde godes sune, seo andswerede and acsode: "Hwu sceal þiss gewurðen? For ic ne cann naht of weres gemane." Gyf ænige mædene þe hæfde gemynt were to underfone, and wære gesæd þæt heo scolde sune geberen ne þuhte hit hire sellic, ne heo axigen nolde: "Hwu sceal hit gewurðen þæt ic sune gebide?" Ac eaðe þeos mihte axigen: "Hwu sceall þiss gewurdeðen þæt ic sune habbe?" For þeh heo Josepe gehandfæst wære, þehhweðere he hæfde anrædlice on hire gemynte, þæt heo næfre weres gemænnysse nolde cunnen.

Emb hire eadmodnysse we mugen eac secgen. Ða þa se ængel hire brohte gretinge fram heofonerice [fol. 153r] and gewiterede heo hwu heo wæs þan hælende to moder gecoren and þehhwæðere gehealdene mægeðhade and gebletsod ofer ealle wifen. Heo andswerede mid eadmodnysse: "Ic eam drihtenes þenen." On oðre stowe heo cwæð: "Drihten, beseh to minre eadmodnysse and þurh þæt me sculen ealle mægðen eadige tellen." Eale hwu heh mæden Godes moder. Hwæt mihte beon herre? Eale hwu eadmode moder Godes þinen. Hwu mihte heo eadmodlucor andswerigen?

Sume næmmeð þone cæstel "Magdalum," þe Maria wæs of Magdalenisc geclypod and þæt becumð wel to þyssere trahtnunge. For Magdalus is stepel geclypod, betacneð eadmodnysse. Here he nis beo name gecyðed, ac is gesæd sum cæstel; and þæt nis na on idel gedon, for sum cæstel þæt is sunderlic cæstel þæt wæs þæt mæden Maria. For þeh manege oðre habben mægeðhades weall and eadmodnyssen stepel swa þæt heo mædene beon and eac eadmode, þehhweðere ne mugen heo gehealde ne mægeðhades modres beon ne bearn geberen swa þeos synderlice dyde. And forþan heo is [folio153v] rihtlice geclypod sum cæstel, þæt is synderlic cæstel, for heo wæs synderlice moder and mæden swa nan oðer ne mihte, ne næfre ma ne mæig. And þeh hit eall gelumpe þæt ænig hæfde þa geðincðe—þæt heo mihte mæden beon and eac cildes moder—þehhweðere ne fullcumð næfre nan to þære mærðe þæt heo þone ilca sune gebere, oððe ægne his gelica. Forþan rihtlice heo is synderlice se ilca cæstel þær ure drihten in com. Þæt geat þær he inn com þæt is hire geleafe. For þurh þæt þæt heo þæs ængles worden gelefde, hit wearð fullfremod on hire þæt þæt se ængel hire sæde.

Ne for þæs hælendes infare næs se cæstel hire mægeðhades ne hire eadmodnyssen gewæmmed, for he is hælend and na awerdend. Þa awerde þing he gehælð and þa gehale he gefæstneð on strencðe. His weorc synden swa swa his name sweigð.

Let us take that gospel as testimony of her virginity and her humility. Then when the angel revealed to her that she would give birth to God's son, she answered and asked: "How shall this come about? I know nothing of a man's company." If any virgin had been minded to take a man, and it were said that she should bear a son and it did not seem strange to her, she would not ask: "How shall if come about that I might expect a son?" But she might easily ask: "How shall *this* come about that I will have a son?" For even though she was engaged to Joseph, nevertheless he been constantly on her mind in that she would never know the company of a man.

About her humility we might say more. Then the angel brought her a greeting from the heaven and informed her how she had been chosen as the mother of the Saviour and even so she would retain her virginity and be blessed above all women. She answered with humility: "I am the handmaid of the Lord." In another place she said: "Lord, behold my humility, and through that shall all virgins count me blessed." Listen to how high a virgin is God's mother. What might be higher? Listen how humble a handmaid is the mother of God. How might she answer more humbly?

Some call the castle "Magdalum," as Mary was named from the Magdalen people, and that fits well with this commentary. For Magdalus is what a tower is called, signifying humility. Here it is not known by this name, but it is called a castle; and that is not done in vain, for that certain castle is a unique castle—that was that Virgin Mary. For though many others have the wall of virginity and the tower of humility so that they are virgins and also humble, nevertheless she might not protect her virginity and be a mother or bear a child as this virgin uniquely did. And so she is rightly called a castle, that is a *unique* castle, for she was uniquely a mother and a virgin as no other might be nor ever will be. And though it entirely happened that someone had that thought—that she might be a virgin and also a child's mother—even so that marvel would never occur such that she could bear that same son or anything like him. Therefore, and rightly, it is uniquely that same castle where our Lord entered. That gate where he came in, that is her faith, for because she believed the angel's words, what the angel had said to her became borne out in her.

The Saviour's entry did not defile the castle of her virginity or her humility, for he is the Saviour and no destroyer. He heals the destroyed thing and the unblemished he secures with strength. His works are just as his name signifies.

Sum wif hine underfeng on hire hus þære wæs Martha to name. Seo hæfde ane suster þe wæs geclypod Maria. Ðas twa gesustre beo þan þe ure larðeawas us [fol. 154r] cyðeð betacnigeð þa twa lif þe man lætt on rihtwisnysse: Martha þæt geswyncfulle lif þe we one drohtnigeð; Maria þæt ece lif þe we to willnigeð. Martha swanc and becarcade to geforðigene þan hælende and his þeowen þa lichamlice behefðen. Maria fæstlice wunede abuten þan hælende and hlyste his worden. Seo studdede emb þa uterlice þing; þeos oðer þa inweardlice þing gemyndelice besceawode.

Swa swa ure hlæfdige is synderlice þæs hælendes moder, swa byð eac synderlice on hire gehealdene þa weorc þære twegre lifen þe þas twa gesustre betacnigeð. On nanre oðre næs Marthe studdinge on nanen time swa fullice geforðed toweard Gode and toweard his leomen, swa on ures drihtenes moder. Ne Marien besceawunge ne hire hlystinge to Godes worden næs næfre on nanre oðre swa fullice geforðed swa on ure drihtenes moder.

Uten nu getrehtnigen Marthen weorc and syððen Mærien sceawunge, and swa þæt we hit þæs [fol. 154v] we openlicor mugen understanden trahtnigen we hwæt oðre halgen wyrceð on Marthen wisen and hwæt þeos; and hwæt oðre halgen behealdeð and hercnigeð on Marie wisen and hwæt þeos.

Oðre underfoð sumne cume leoflice for þæs hælendes lufe, ac þeos nænne oðerne cume bute þone hælend sylf, na synderlice on oðren herbyrge, bute on hire agene innoðe. Oðre bescrydeð sumne hnacodne mid ateorigendlicen reafe, ac þeos gelichamede Godes ungeseowenlicne sune mid clænen and unbesmitenen lichame, þe næfre on ecnysse ne sceareð ne ne for roteð, ac on unwæmme þurhwuneð. Oðre fedeð sumne hungrigne oððe þurstigne mid uterlicen mete oððe drænce, ac þeos na feorlucor bute of hire agene breostes meolca fedde and fostrode þone þe is God and mann þa þa he wæs on mænniscen gecynde hungrig and þurstig.

And swa swa we hit mugen scortlice belucan ealla þa six mildheortnysse weorcas þe God geopeneð on domesdæige loc [fol. 155r] hwænne he cweðð: "Eall þæt þæt ge dydon anen minre læsten þæt ge dyden me sylfen"; ealla þa ilca heo dyde synderlice and furðerlucor þone ænig oðer, na on ænigen oðren lytlen, ac on þan sylfen Godes sunen. Swa swa leofne gyst heo hine husede and innlice herebyregode. Ðonne he hnacod wæs, heo hine beswreah mid lichame and mid reafe. Ðonne he wæs hungrig and þurstige, heo hine estlice gefylde mid hire meolca. On his cildlicen unsernysse, heo hine baðede and beðede, and smerede and bær, and frefrede and swaðede and roccode. Swa þæt man mæig rihtlice beon hire secgen, Martha wæs bisig and cearig emb þa þenunge.

A certain woman, whose name was Martha, received him into her house. She had a sister called Mary. These two sisters are those, who as our teachers reveal to us, signify the two lives which are permitted to a person in righteousness: Martha is that active life which we now live; Mary that eternal life which we desire. Martha laboured and was anxious to take care of the Saviour and serve his physical needs. Mary resolutely stayed around the Saviour and listened to his words. The one troubled about outer things; the other thoughtfully contemplated spiritual things.

Just as our lady is uniquely the mother of the Saviour, so in her is also uniquely represented the work of the two lives which the two sisters symbolize. In no other, at any time, was Martha's eager effort as fully accomplished towards God and towards his physical being as it was by our Lord's mother. Nor was Mary's contemplation nor her listening to God's word ever in any way as fully accomplished as by our Lord's mother.

Let us now explain Martha's work and then Mary's contemplation, and so that we may more clearly understand we will explain what other holy people perform in the manner of Martha, and what these are; and what other holy people observe and hear in the manner of Mary, and what these are.

Some receive any guest willingly for the love of the Saviour, but for her, there was no other guest except the Saviour himself, not separately in another lodging, but in her own womb. Some clothe a naked person with perishable clothing, but she clothed with flesh God's unseen son with a pure and undefiled body, which will never throughout eternity be damaged or decay, but will remain undefiled. Some fed some hungry or thirsty person with external food or drink, but it was no further from her own breast's milk that she fed and nourished him, who is God and man, when he was hungry and thirsty in the manner of humankind.

And so we might briefly define all the six merciful works which God will reveal at the conclusion of Judgement Day, when he says: "All that you did for the least of one of mine you did for me myself"; and all of those same things she did specially and more so than any other, not for any unimportant person, but for God's son himself. So just like a beloved guest she housed him and harboured him inwardly. When he was naked, she wrapped him with a body and clothed him; when he was hungry and thirsty, she graciously filled him with her milk. In his childhood sickness, she bathed him, and warmed him, and anointed him, and carried him, and comforted him, and swaddled him, and rocked him. So a person may rightly say about her, Martha was busy and troubled about service to others.

Ða þa he wæs genumen and on rode gefestned, swa swa on cwarterne gedon, þær heo com, swa swa hit awriten is: "Big þæs hælendes rode stod Maria his moder." Onmang þyssen þingen heo wæs bisig and gedrefd: gedrefd heo wæs þa þa heo fleah into Egypte for Herode kinge þe hire cild wolde fordon; gedrefd heo wæs þa þa heo understood þæt þæt [fol. 155v] Iudeisce folc wiðsette hire sune to deaðe. Æt þan ænde heo wæs inlice gedrefod, and swa swa Symeon hire hwilen ær gewitegode, his slege þurheode hire sawle þa þa heo geseh hire swylcne sune nymen, binden and swingan, and bespæten his ansene. Cynehelmigen hine mid þornen, earplættigen, and on rode fæstnigen sweltan and bebyrigen. Beo hire man mæg rihtlice secgen: "Martha, Martha, þu eart bisig and gedrefed on feala þingan."

Ne tweonige nane mæn þæt seo gedrefde moder nolde beon gescild wið þære gedrefednysse, and þæt hire sune gyf him gewill wære hire gehulpe mid þære godcunden strængðe þe heo on him wyste, þe betacneð Marie Magdalene. Ðæt betacneð þæt Martha bemænde to þan hælende þæt heo næfde fultum of hire suster to þan lichamlicen geswynce, þiss is Marthe dæl. Ac hwa mæig swa wurðlice swa hit gebyrede gereccen hwu herigendlice is on þære eadigen Cristes moder Marien dæl [fol. 156r] þæt þæt se hælend herede. Syððen hit is swa swa we sæden and betere þone we sæden on þæs hælendes moder Marthan geswyncfulle wica þe se hælend naht herode, ac þehhweðere he hit na ne tælde. Hwylc wæs on hire þæt dæl þe Maria geceas þe ure drihten herede and cwæð þæt hit selest wære, and heo eac eadig for hit næfre hire ne wurde benumen.

Eala, hwu mycel swotnysse wæs mid þære eadige cwen þa þa se halge gast on hire becom, and þæs hecsten mihte heo bescadewode swa þæt heo of þan ilcan halgen gaste wearð bearneacninde. Hwæt wanode hire of Godes wisedome þa þa inne hire lutede eall Godes wisedom, and God sylf on hire innoðe timbrede himsylfen mænnisc lichame? Se apostel Paulus cwæð: "On Criste synd beclysede Godes mihten and his wisedom and ealle þa hordwittes and wisedomes, and Crist on Marien and swa is Godes mihte and his wisedom and ealle þa hordwittes and wisedomes on Marien."

Ðeos sæt wel þan hælende æt [fol. 156v] foten and æt heafde hlystinde his worden. Heo understood ealle þa word þære ænglen and þære herdan, and þære tungelwitegan and eac forðen þæs sylfen hælendes and heold gemyndelice on hire heorte. Næfre ær ne æfter nan oðer swa forðlice ne gesmæhte hwu swote is ure drihten. Heo wæs wel beo þæs witegan cwide þurhdrænct mid þære welle Godes huse, and of þan streamen his esten hire wæs wel gescænct. þæt næs nan wunder for innen hire wæs se rihte spryng þære lifes welle, þær offlowð eall seo fullfremednysse þære twegre lifen þe we embe specað.

When he was seized and fastened on the rood, just as he was put in prison, there she came, just as it is written "By the Saviour's Cross stood Mary his mother." Among other things she was busy and troubled: troubled she was when she fled into Egypt because King Herod wanted to kill her child; troubled she was when she perceived that the Jewish people condemned her son to death. At the end she was inwardly troubled, and just as Simon had revealed to her a while before, his death pierced her soul when she saw her son seized like that, bound and scourged, and his face spat on. They crowned him with thorns, hit him about the ears, and fastened him on the cross to die and be buried. About her a person might rightly say: "Martha, Martha, you are busy and troubled about many things."

No person should doubt that the troubled mother would not be protected against this affliction, and that her son, if it was his will, would help her with the divine strength which she knew to be in him, which signifies Mary Magdalen. That betokens what Martha lamented to the Saviour that she did not have help from her sister in the labours of the body: this is Martha's part. But who can relate as honourably as is fitting how excellent is the part of Mary, mother of the blessed Christ, that the Saviour praised. Afterwards, it is just as we said and better than we said about the Saviour's mother, the painful part of Martha that the Saviour did not praise at all, but yet he did not reproach it. Such was in her that part which Mary chose which our Lord praised and said that it was best, and she is also blessed because it will never be taken away from her.

Oh, how much sweetness was in that blessed queen when the holy spirit came to her, and she contemplated the highest power so that she became pregnant through that same holy spirit. What did she lack of God's wisdom when within her hid all of God's wisdom, and within her womb God himself built himself a man's body. The apostle Paul said: "In Christ is confined God's power and his wisdom, and in Mary is Christ, and so God's power and his wisdom and all his virtue and wisdom is in Mary."

This woman sat content by the Saviour at his feet and at his head listening to his words. She understood all the words of the angels and the shepherds, and the wise men, and also of the Saviour himself and retained them in fully in her heart. Never before nor after has any other so thoroughly tasted how sweet our Lord is. She was saturated completely, as the prophet said, with the well of God's house, and the stream of his grace was poured out on her. This was no wonder because within her was the righteous spring of life's well, from which overflows all the perfection of the two lives that we spoke about.

Emb feala þing heo wæs swa swa Martha, bisig and cearig. Anlypig þing hire wæs este and gemynde swa swa Marian, for an þing is beheflic. Þa feala þing hire byð wiðtogene, þæt an hire is belæfd. Forþan we secgeð þæt heo synderlice fullforðede Marthen geswyncfulle wica, and synderlice heo gehealt þæt seleste Marien dæl. Ac hire is Marthe dæl benumen. For heo nis na [fol. 157r] læng bisig to fostrigen hire sune swa swa cilde, nu him þenigeð ænglena werod swa swa hlaforde. Nu ne carcað heo to befleon Herodes ehtnysse into Egypte mid hire cilde. For he is gestogan into heofone, and Herodes is beflogen his ansyne into helle þeostre. Nu nis heo na mare gedrefd for þære Iudean ehtnysse toweard hire sune for ealle þing him synd underðeodde. Ne sculen na mare þa Iudees hire sune swingan ne cwellen, for he is arisen of deaðe, and ne swelt næfre ma. Heonenforð næfð se deað nænne styde on him.

Ðuss hire is Marthen geswyncfulle lif eall ætbroigden, and to hire freome hire is Marie dæl belæfd þæt hire næfre ne byð benumen. For heo is upahafen ofer ænglene werod and eall hire wille hire is geforðed on godnysse, for heo gesihð hire sune eall ealswa he is. Ðiss is þe seleste dæl þæt hit næfre ne byð hir wiðtogen; þæs dæles us geunne God þurh hire þingunge þæt we beon dælnymende þurh his mildheortnysse.

[fol. 157v] We wylleð eow nu bi sum dæl gereccen emben hyre neamagen þe hire besibbe wæron. Anna[38] and Emeria wæron gesustre. On Emeria wæs geboren Elisabeth, Iohannes moder þæs fulhteres. Of Anna wæs geboren Maria Cristes moder, and þa þa hire were Ioachim wæs forðfaren þa genam Anna, æfter Moyses æ, oðerne were þe wæs genæmd Cleophas. Of þan heo hæfde an oðre dohter, seo wæs eac genæmd Maria, æfter þære ærre dohter. þas man cleopeð Maria Cleophe for heo wæs his dohter.

Ða beweddede Cleophas Iosephe his broðre Marian, þæs hælendes moder, þe wæs his steopdohter; and his agene dohter Marian he geaf Alpheon. Of þære wæs geboren Iacob se læsse and se oðer Ioseph. Ðes Iacob wæs geclypod Iacobus Alphei for he wæs Alphees sune.

Ða get æfter Cleophas deaðe, Anna, æfter þære lage, genam þone þridde were þan wæs to name Salomas. Of him [fol. 158r] heo hæfde þa þridde dohter, and heo genæmden eac Marien for þære deorewurðnysse of þære forme dohter, and forþanþe se ængel brohte þone name. Seo wæs bewedded Zebedeo, of þære wæron geborene Iacob se mycele and Iohannes se godspellere. Maria þæs læsse Iacobes moder and Maria þæs mare Iacobes moder and Iohannes þæs godspelleres and Maria seo Magdalenissce sohten urne drihten mid smerigeles inne his þruge þa þa he bebyriged wæs.

38 This short new text is introduced not only by the introductory clause at the top of fol. 157v, but by an elaborate large offset initial **A** in green and red.

About many things she was just like Martha, busy and troubled. About one thing was her grace and mind, just like Mary, for just the one thing is necessary. The many things are taken away from her so that one thing remained to her. Therefore, we say that she uniquely accomplished Martha's laborious lodging, and she especially held onto Mary's best part. But Martha's part will be taken away from her. For she will not be anxious for too long to nurse her son as a child, whom all the hosts of angels now serve as their Lord. She will not be anxious to flee from Herod's sight into Egypt with her child, for he has now ascended into heaven, and Herod has descended from his sight into the darkness of hell. She will be no longer troubled because of the Jews' persecution towards her son for all things are subjected to him. No more shall the Jews flog or kill her son, for he is risen from death and will never more die. From now on, death will have no power over him.

Thus in her is Martha's laborious life all carried away, and to her benefit Mary's part remains and will never be taken away from her. For she is lifted up over the host of angels and all her desire is fulfilled in goodness, for she sees her son entirely as he is. This is the best part that will never be taken away from her; of this part God grants us through her service that we shall participate through his mercy.

[*Trinubium Annae*] Now we want to tell you in part about those who were related to her. Anna and Emeria were sisters. From Emeria, Elizabeth, the mother of John the Baptist, was born. From Anna, Mary, the mother of Christ, was born, and then when her husband Joachim had passed away, following Moses's law, Anna took another husband, who was called Cleophas. From that, she had another daughter, who was also called Mary, after the first daughter. Mary is called Mary Cleophas because she was his daughter.

Then Cleophas had his brother Joseph marry Mary, the Saviour's mother, who was his stepdaughter; and he gave his own daughter Mary to Alpheon. From her, James the Lesser and the other Joseph were born. This James was called James Alpheus because he was the son of Alpheus.

Then further, after Cleophas' death, Anna, following the law, took a third husband, whose name was Salomas. By him, she had a third daughter, and they also named her Mary because of the preciousness of the first daughter, and because the angel brought her the name. She married Zebedee, and from her James the Greater and John the Evangelist were born. Mary, the mother of James the Lesser, and Mary, the mother of the James the Greater and John the Evangelist, and Mary Magdalene then sought our Lord with ointment in his tomb when he was buried.

Chapter 3

LIFE AND DEATH

TRANSITION AND TRANSFORMATION

JUST AS the D'Escures homily examined in Chapter 2 raises key issues about categories of language, of scholarly period, and of English literature worth studying, so this chapter will highlight similar themes in its focus on the short poem, *The Grave*, contained in the bilingual manuscript, Oxford, Bodleian Library, MS Bodley 343, edited and translated below. Dated to about 1180–1200, this poem is a vibrant and sensual account of the decaying corpse in its grave, a grave predetermined before birth. The poem has recently attracted scholarly attention, partly for its dynamism, and partly for its significant place in the literature from this period. It seems unique in looking back to "Old" English alliterative poetic and thematic traditions, and yet it clearly heralds "Middle" English lyricism and individualism. It sits between literatures, then, and even languages—at least between categories that modern scholarship solidifies within the academy and in publishing. In this chapter I will show how the poem disrupts boundaries, rather than reinforcing them, and how, in the process of doing so, it urges readers to think again about the old and the new, death and life.

Thousands of medieval manuscripts and early printed books are filled with interventions that were never part of the intentional book's design. And thousands more premodern books are filled with annotations and commentary, glosses and reading cues that are directly related to the intentional text, and for which space was often left in between lines (interlinearly) or in generous margins (marginally). This chapter will focus on writing entered into a book that was certainly an afterthought—written down perhaps because the original text prompted a reaction in the reader-writer, or simply because blank membrane encouraged the writer to enter their thoughts. A second writer then added a further short set of thoughts in an effort, it seems, to finish off the poem. Intervention into part of a blank folio can appear in the guise of conversation when a later annotator adds notes or comments; sometimes the annotator will criticize or overwrite a message in the earlier text.[1] Given the way in which manuscripts could start life as booklets, small books, or larger textual productions; or could exist in a temporary vellum

1 See Hill, "Two Micro-Texts in Ælfric's *Catholic Homilies*."

binding before being bound with other book(let)s into something larger; or could be found in various states of repair or disrepair and rebound in the early modern period or later, little notes and comments added to the margins or flyleaves can seem inconsequential, but they are often poetic or proverbial, augmenting the texts they surround. They ask us to reconsider the nineteenth-century aestheticization of the category of "literary."[2] It could be argued that anything that is written should be considered "literature," just as the word's use in English in the late Middle Ages initially signified, since *littera* means simply "letters." In the last two centuries, "literature" has taken on connotations of artistry and prestige, and a question that arises from this hierarchical perspective is whether literature must, then, always be a *central* text, or a major text? If so, *The Grave*, with its brevity and marginal status may not attain that modern status. Short lyrics or alliterative verselines added in pencil to the endleaves of manuscripts would be "jottings" or "scribbles." Yet, these brief poetic moments do speak to emotion, wit, and the desire to convey thought and feeling sensitively and often with a visible poeticism. This does not simply concern short texts either, for within this aesthetic hierarchy, whole genres can be dismissed as unliterary. Hagiography and homilies, and sermons themselves are often considered to be barely "literary" in the way that a medieval romance or secular fiction and lyric might be, and especially texts that are written in prose for pragmatic or didactic ends. Still, as texts in the later twelfth-century codex Oxford, Bodleian Library, MS Bodley 343 will illustrate, religious prose and poetry can hold their own with any other literature, even texts that are Literary with a capital "L."

Dead Things Speak

From folio 163, line 13, of the extensive English and Latin homiletic manuscript, Bodley 343, is a prose sermon that its nineteenth-century editor, A. O. Belfour, entitled "A Message from the Tomb."[3] Part-Wulfstan (the eleventh-century archbishop of York; writer and statesman) and part-anonymous adaptation of a homily by the early theologian, Caesarius of Arles, the admo-

---

2 See Treharne, *Perceptions of Medieval Manuscripts*, Chapter 3.

3 On Bodley 343, see Conti, "Preaching Scripture and Apocrypha." As well as Belfour's edition of this and other homilies in Belfour, *Twelfth-Century Homilies*, Irvine also edits this homily with an emphasis on its sources. It is her number VII, "The Transience of Earthly Delights," in *Old English Homilies*, 178–204. In her description of this composite homily, at 181, she unfortunately describes the work of the scribe-compiler as "slavish copying."

nition to focus on the last things—death and judgement—seeks to remind the living to dispense with the transitory things of this world that are like "monnes sceadu" ("a person's shadow").[4] The audience is asked to acknowledge the decaying body of someone they formerly knew, and consider what "þa ðyrle ban" ("the fretted bones") and "þæs deadan dust of þare buriȝnes" ("the dust of the dead person in that grave") might say to the passerby, if only bones and dust could speak ("þeah þe ða deade ban of þare buriȝnes specon ne maȝon"—"though the dead bones cannot speak from the grave"). The bones warn all to avoid covetousness, pride, sinfulness, reminding the audience that they too shall end up as porous skeletons. A lively account of Doomsday, with fiery heavens, crackling flame, and a stern company of Christ and his angels leads into an exposition of the "*Ubi Sunt*?" motif, which asks where those are who have gone before, and reacquaints the reader-listener with a favourite theme of earlier writers—the transient nature of human life.

This Latin and English homiliary, Bodley 343, was produced ca. 1180 somewhere in the West Midlands area and was created as reference for preachers and religious teachers, for pastoral care, and didactic and liturgical instruction. It thus sought to ensure the salvation of its readers and listeners, who may have had varied competencies and levels of education. The later addition to the manuscript of musical texts creates something rather more multifunctional of the codex as a whole, as Chapter 4 will discuss, intimating a specifically liturgical purpose, though sermons like those in Bodley 343 were a regular part of the liturgy in the English church anyway.

The manuscript is usually ascribed an origin of Worcester Cathedral Priory, though it is rather unlike other Worcester manuscripts in this period. Moreover, it is not obviously written, annotated, or glossed by the famous scribe, the Tremulous Hand. This scribe, operating between ca. 1190 and 1225 is often (but without incontrovertible evidence) linked to Worcester because they wrote in other English manuscripts with a medieval origin or provenance of Worcester, like Oxford, Bodleian Library, MSS Hatton 113, 114, 115, and 116.

Bodley 343's palaeographical and codicological evidence hints, actually, at a place of origin other than Worcester.[5] It has unusual capital letters which are black and red with geometric or foliate decoration includ-

4 Ultimately derived from Caesarius of Arles's *De Elemosinis*, as discussed by Irvine, *Old English Homilies*, 183.

5 As suggested some years ago, indeed, by Kitson, "Old English Dialects." He thought Hereford to be a possibility and I agree.

ing an idiosyncratic hand-like lobe to the floriation that is seen sporadically through the manuscript. It may be linked with London, British Library, Cotton MS Claudius E. i, made at Tewkesbury in the late twelfth and earlier thirteenth centuries.[6] The veneration of St. Wulfstan indicated by an image of him added later in Bodley 343 intimates Tewkesbury, too, since it had a particular devotion to that saint, but there is also significant reason to believe Hereford to be the place of origin. This evidence for the manuscript as a whole will be discussed in greater detail in the following chapter when I turn to scribes and scribal practices in this period. In this chapter, I shall be focused principally on the poem known as *The Grave.*

Perhaps inspired by the homiletic context of Bodley 343, sometime after the completion of the main homiliary two scribes entered a poem in two stages into the nine blank lines of fol. 170r, after the end of the final English homily in the manuscript, which was the closing text of the main scribal effort. This short, dense poem, *The Grave*, has until recently been seen as a rather obscure and poorly thought of set of verse-lines focused on what happens to the body after death. In the last two decades it has been re-positioned within the context of post-Conquest English literary production.[7] It was included in my 2009 *Old and Middle English Anthology*; and it has been discussed by a number of scholars in recent essay collections.[8] I began work on this poem long ago with a view to using the later twelfth-century English *Grave* as a metaphor for the contemporary demise of literary culture traditionally labelled as *Old* English. The poem emerges at precisely the moment when we might imagine the earliest English transforms into what has become commonly labelled as Middle English. Yet *The Grave* is a poem that simultaneously looks backward to pre-Conquest traditions of Body and Soul literature, alliterative lyrical expression, and doctrinal wisdom, while also looking forward to post-Conquest subjectivity and to twelfth-century realism, devotional focus, and lively didacticism. The problem of periodization as a mode of intellectual organization (as discussed in earlier chapters) is illustrated by this poem's refusal to be either wholly novel or nostalgic. There is no doubt that this poem is as well composed, packed with emphasis

---

6 This manuscript is fully digitized on the British Library's digital manuscripts website.

7 This analysis of *The Grave* was first given at the University of Leeds International Medieval Congress 2013, where I benefitted from discussion with Professors Chris Jones (University of Utah) and Thomas Bredehoft. I am grateful to my undergraduate students at Stanford, whose curiosity about *The Grave* has helped my own thoughts become clearer.

8 Such as Jones, "Re-lining *The Grave*."

and emotion, as any other shorter poem from the longue durée of English literary history. It is as compelling, as engaging and as evocative a text as one is likely to read. This was recognized by several great figures in literature, from Alfred, Lord Tennyson, to Jorge Luis Borges.

The Grave had been undervalued in the English literary canon because it is more nebulous than many works that are frequently taught and read: it does not fit. All the reasons for ascribing negative value judgements to it seemed to pertain: it has no known author and no substantiated date of origin: the end of the twelfth or beginning of the thirteenth centuries is its purported date range, or just "later" than its manuscript context in Bodley 343—itself written in the late decades of the twelfth century. It is certainly "copied" in as much as there are scribal emendations showing there was an exemplar in front of the initial scribe. Whether that exemplar was much older or whether it was a freshly written draft of the poem, we shall never know. In addition, there was no agreed upon text of the poem, since the last line-and-a-half of the poem in its manuscript setting are written in a shaky hand that certainly appear to be a little later than the first thirteen lines. The poem was published in varied forms and regarded—without any evidence to support this—as being a fragment. Perhaps because of these uncertainties, it is the perfect example of an English poetic text of its day; it appears to be an afterthought, regional, peripheral—as are so many lyrics in this period, slipped into the margins and spaces of their host manuscripts.[9] Yet, while this addition is dynamic, innovative, and well-constructed, it is not actually a fragment; it is complete (in fact, it is *twice* completed). It is not a piece of marginalia added because of the convenience and potential for expression of the folio's space; it is thoroughly and thoughtfully integrated into the homiletic context of the manuscript. *The Grave* provides a sign of a different kind of devotional and didactic work in this period through its notable originality. At this point, too, it seems that the poetic mode became of even greater significance in a liturgical setting; direct and emotive appeal to the individual helped reinforce the rather more distant or institutional feel of the prose sermon, dozens of which *precede The Grave* in Bodley 343.

As a text added to preceding works in an expert but rather irregular hand, in a language where the so-called "standard" forms of the tenth and eleventh centuries are beginning to dissipate, *The Grave* also perfectly exem-

9 See, Aiello, "English Vernacular Script." For an example, see Cambridge Corpus Christi College, MS 188, page 408, where the lyrical verse "þine mot ihc gon meyde swete / lefwine mot hi" has been added in a thirteenth-century *textura* (book) hand at the bottom of the folio containing eleventh-century English homilies.

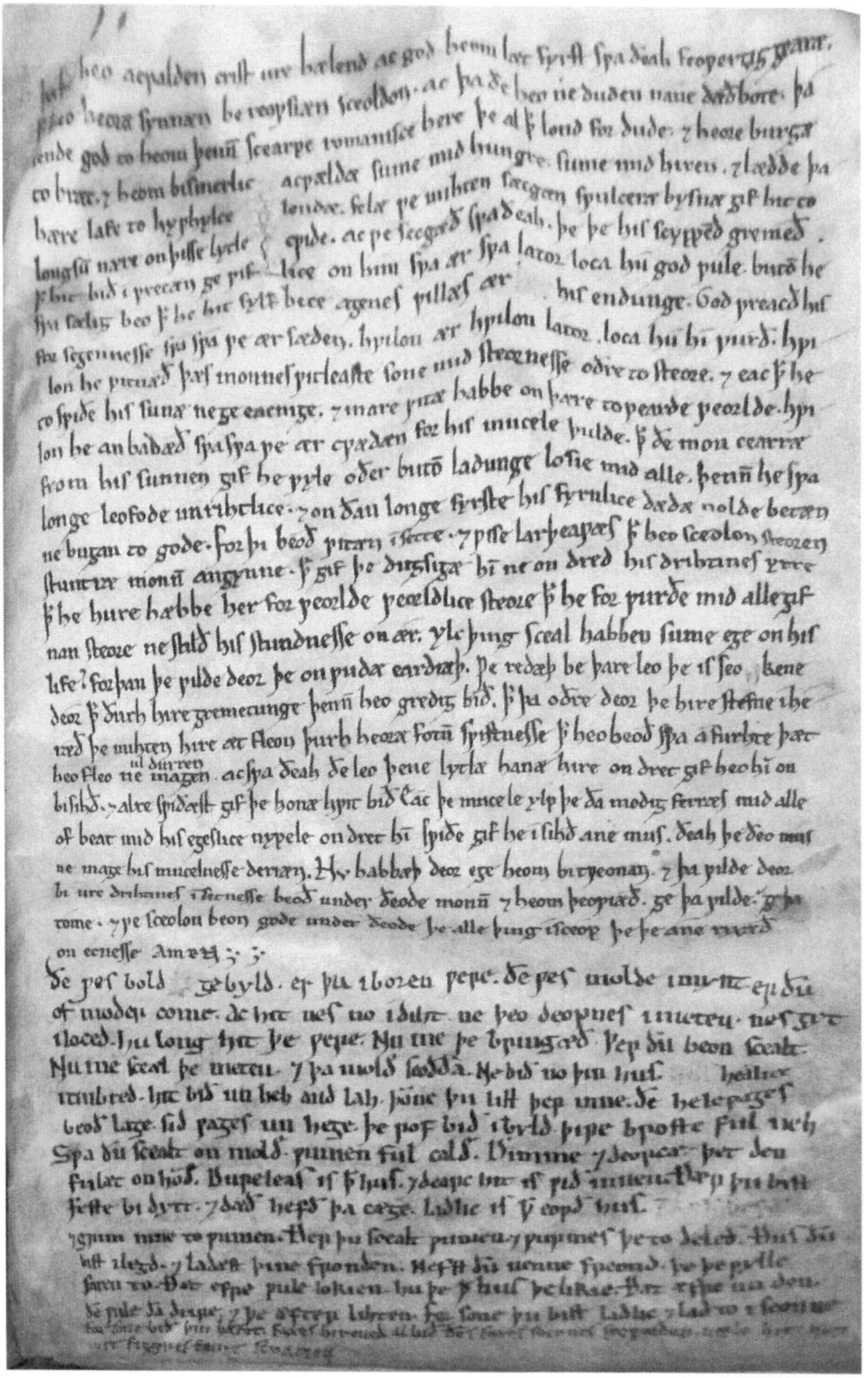

Figure 4. Oxford, Bodleian Library, Bodley MS 343, fol. 170r.
Photograph by the author. © The Bodleian Library, Oxford.

plifies core issues for medieval literary scholars:[10] the importance of the codicological, scribal, and linguistic, and the role of anticipated and actual *function* of these early texts. The very existence of this short, dense work, as other texts in this manuscript also show, suggests the need for a reassessment of manuscripts containing English from 1170–1250 in parallel with Latin and French comparators, to create a better understanding of writing practices and the role of multilingual scribes. This period, when late Caroline Minuscule script evolved into what is commonly labelled Gothic in Latin manuscripts, is also key to the development of other forms of script (like the more cursive category of script that emerges and which was labelled *Anglicana* by N. R. Ker in 1962) often employed in the vernaculars. In addition, innovation in the layout of books and the *size* of writing emerges at this key point, as scholastic influences become more important in book production.[11] A full and detailed analysis of linguistic data from ca. 1150–1250 is also overdue, using all English materials accompanied by comparison with other languages in Britain at this time. Such analyses have been in progress for years under the auspices of the *Linguistic Atlas of Early Medieval English* and various other corpora projects, but overviews have yet to emerge.[12] That is, the data exists, but has not been thoroughly exploited.[13] Such an investigation of linguistic form might not to be too concerned with dialect in the first instance, but instead could concentrate on a detailed description of language use in texts to further research in descriptive features, dating, and to assess the utility of traditional boundaries of interpretation—categories, like dialect, scribal hands, the concept of originality, and questions of completeness.

Finally, a reassessment of book categorizations or genres would be a useful exercise, particularly in the light of the availability of many more manuscripts in digital form. Most manuscript and literary historians label books taking cues from the manuscript compiler's ostensible intentional-

10 On standard Old English, see Hofstetter, "Winchester and the Standardization of Old English." It should be said that no individual manuscript of Early English rigidly conforms to the theoretical "standard." The privileging of this standard has led to the derogation of many scribes whose orthography and accidence is inconsistent or "non-standard."

11 On this, see Aiello, "English Vernacular Script"; and Parkes, *English Cursive Book Hands*."

12 Laing, *Catalogue of Sources*; Blake, *The Cambridge History of the English Language*; Lass, *Old English*.

13 Mark Faulkner at Trinity College, Dublin, is investigating language and language change in his project, "Searobend."

ity; so, for example, a book with homilies is a preacher's book; a book with texts like debates, encyclopaedic works, or with items that show signs of glossing is a teacher's book; a book with an assortment of religious texts is a devotional book, and so forth. All manuscript books are, though, effectively long-living, multifunctional, and often diversified by texts that are added. Contemporary and later users' marks of engagement can show how they understood the books they were inscribing. As such, in their specific temporal moments of production and use, books retain their wholeness but are clearly never thought of as "complete." While the book's multifunctionality may not always be detectable, since users of books often do not always leave obvious marks,[14] where users do leave traces these might suggest many passers-through or only one annotator writing at different times; or, where there are only sporadic traces, these might nonetheless intimate an intense and earnest interest in the texts of the book. Where users intervene independently in the book—adding words or images that are, to us at least, not related to the pre-existing body of text—this necessarily suggests a shift in the function of the codex and it raises important questions about the relationship of the user to the book. We need to be alive to all these nuances in our approaches.

My view is that the "multifunctional" book typifies twelfth- and thirteenth-century English vernacular activity. Modern responses to these manuscripts cataloguing the contents, or labelling the book as of a particular type, constrain the interpretative potential. It is only recently that scholars have begun to spend careful time deeply investigating the making, materiality, and continual use of medieval books without pre-judgement. And from just one example studied within its broader manuscript context—*The Grave* in Bodley 343—it is possible to see how confining labels and preconceptions about textual production can be. *The Grave*, when extrapolated from the manuscript setting in which it was composed as it generally is in editions and scholarly analysis seems far more anomalous or out-of-place than it is.

14 Or those marks have been erased or washed away, as, for example, with Aberystwyth, National Library of Wales, Peniarth MS 392D—the famous Hengwrt Chaucer, datable to ca. 1400, and possibly the earliest surviving copy of the *Canterbury Tales*. Work by Andrew Prescott and me, following earlier research by Estelle Stubbs, suggests marginal annotation and scribal cues have been erased.

Engraving Death

The verse copied as long lines onto fol. 170r of Oxford, Bodleian Library, Bodley MS 343 in the closing years of the twelfth century were published first as "Death Speaks" by J. J. Conybeare in 1814 from a letter he had written to Henry Ellis in 1811. Here the poem appears minus the last three lines. Conybeare edited it alongside his own Latin translation and an English translation, commenting that it is one of the last of the earliest English poems and rare in this period:

> This short composition appears to present a specimen, not altogether uninteresting, of our language and poetry, at the latest period at which they could fairly be denominated Saxon. Productions of this æra are not (either in print or in manuscript) of very frequent occurrence.[15]

The three-column layout of Conybeare's printing of the text results in the poem's presentation in half-lines.

<table>
<tr><td>The wes bold ȝebyld</td><td>Tibi fuit domus exstructa</td><td>For thee was a house built</td></tr>
<tr><td>Er ðu iboren were,</td><td>Priusquam natus es,</td><td>Ere thou wert born,</td></tr>
<tr><td>The wes molde imynt</td><td>Tibi fuit tellus parata</td><td>For thee was a mould shapen</td></tr>
<tr><td>Er ðu of moder come</td><td>Priusquam e matre venisti.</td><td>Ere thou of mother camest.[16]</td></tr>
</table>

The focus of Conybeare's edition is the alliteration of the English verse and the connection he sees between this poem and pre-Conquest poetry. He further observes, though, that the poem, appearing to be "inferior in regularity both of numbers and alliteration to the earlier specimens of Saxon-Poetry preserved to us by the labours of Hickes and Junius," is to be dated after the Norman Conquest.[17] Conybeare's desire to accommodate this poem as a late *Old* English composition highlights the continuities in verse-form that he perceived; the Latin accompaniment simply indicates the scholarly context of this letter and Conybeare offers no explanation for its intended function.

In his *Analecta Anglo-Saxonica*, published in 1846, Benjamin Thorpe gave the poem its name and declared *The Grave* "this singularly impressive

---

15 Conybeare, "Communication of an inedited Fragment"; Conybeare, *Six Articles on Anglo-Saxon Poetry*, 270–73 (as "Norman-Saxon Fragment on Death"). He comments that Humfrey Wanley thought the poem "to have been written about the time of King Henry the second." See also Schroer, "The Grave"; Rieger, *Alt- und Angelsächsisches Lesebuch*, 124–25; Buchholz, *Die Fragmente*, 11–12; and Conlee, *Middle English Debate Poetry*, 4–5.

16 At 174, Conybeare prints wyn for <w> in the early English. In his translation of line 4, he adds "(thy)" before "mother."

17 Conybeare, "Communication of an Inedited Fragment," 173.

and almost appalling fragment."[18] Like Conybeare, Thorpe printed the poem in half-lines, so that, as immediately below, lines 1, 2, 3, 4, etc. are on the left, with the later lines of the poem on the right. The poem appears rather confusingly in these two non-contiguous columns:

Ðe wes bold ȝebyld	þonne þu list þerinne;
er ðu iboren were,	ðe hele-waȝes beoð lage,
ðe wes molde imynt	sid-wages unhege,
er ðu of moder come;	þe rof bið ibyld
ac hit nes no idiht,	þire broste ful neh;
ne þeo deopnes imeten;	swa ðu scealt on mold
nes gyt iloced,	wunien ful cald,
hu long hit þe were.	dimme and deorcaæ:
Nu me þe bringæð	þet den fulæt on hond.
þer ðu beon scealt;	Dureleas is þæt hus,
nu me sceal þe meten,	and dearc his is wiðinnen,
and ða mold seoðða…	ðær þu bist feste bidytt…

This layout creates, at first glance, a text that would be misleading (indeed, false) for modern readers who are used to reading Early English verse as edited since the nineteenth century; that is, in long lines of two half-lines alliterating across the caesura or space in the middle, which in Thorpe is simply a lacuna separating the columnar layout. Thorpe eliminates the long verse line's alliteration by switching to this format of half-lines written in vertical sequence. In reality, of course, English alliterative verse was rarely laid out in poetic lines in manuscripts prior to ca. 1200, so neither Thorpe nor contemporary editors are providing readers with an experience commensurate with the manuscripts' original.[19]

Even at this point in the transmission of the text, though, the parameters of investigation and identification were set by Conybeare, Thorpe, and other early editors. It is these same parameters that have bounded the twelfth and earlier thirteenth centuries as a whole. Thus, the dating of texts is notoriously difficult after 1150; identification of scribes and determin-

---

18 Thorpe, *Analecta Anglo-Saxonica*, xi; he printed the poem as "The Grave" at 153–54. See p. v of the 1868 edition of *Analecta Anglo-Saxonica* for Thorpe's comments that: "About the Anglo-Saxon tongue there was the strength of iron, with the sparkling and the beauty of burnished steel, which made it withstand with success the attacks that the Norman William and his fawning courtiers directed against it, as they tried in vain to thrust their French into the mouths of the English people." This hyperbolic, nationalist rhetoric is typical of the founders of the field of Early English literature and history.

19 See Weiskott, *English Alliterative Verse*.

ing the limits of scribal activity is problematic; determining how to categorize a text—as Old or Middle English, or neither—means the literary work is lost in the gap;[20] and judging the quality of these texts is accomplished against a before-or-after aesthetic, such that there is little sense of the literature being read on its own merits. With some notable exceptions, such as Laȝamon's *Brut*, then, the literature in the two hundred years from ca. 1050 to ca. 1250 is described as either a deterioration of that which came before or an embryonic example of that which will become more developed.

In addition, when textual additions to manuscripts are ignored or misunderstood, scholars do a disservice to the evidence presented by the object itself: its phenomenological significance as an object-in-the-world. For the scribe(s) of *The Grave*, a form of completion of the manuscript was desirable; the scribe saw the space of the manuscript as an opportunity. The poem written into Bodley 343 was integrated physically onto the same folio as the final in-place homily, and it was integrated thematically with themes of the Last Things running through the Latin and English homilies in the manuscript.

Since the mid-nineteenth century, the poem has been the subject of a dozen or so published studies, few of which have tried to evaluate the work in its own milieu, even when the authors asserted that they would do precisely that. Carolynn Friedlander, in her study of accentual verse, sees *The Grave* (and the *Worcester Fragments*) as "accumulations of clichés" in which "reiteration of the obvious sometimes makes them grimly effective," though none offers "any new development of its traditions."[21] She attributes the development of early Middle English verse to a conscious nostalgia by those "who regret the passing of an age" who are thus "likely to idealize it, and hence to simplify it."[22] There are many problems with this interpretation; principally, there is no real tradition to which one could attribute *The Grave* in terms of its combination of form, style, and perspective. It is multipurpose: a verse homily, but singularly and dramatically poetic, not remotely clichéd (how could it be so when it is almost the only surviving English lyrical poem from an entire century?); it is not Old English, and neither is it "obvious" nor nostalgic, since its themes of an explicit dying were dramatically and differently deployed both before its moment of composition, and long after.

Similarly, Fulk and Cain in their *History of Old English* assert the poem to be part of "Soul and Body" literature, copied at two points—ca. 1150 and ca. 1200—and considered both Old and Middle English. Describing it

---

20 Treharne, *Living Through Conquest*.

21 Friedlander, "Early Middle English Accentual Verse," 227.

22 Friedlander, "Early Middle English Accentual Verse," 230.

as "probably...a fragment" and "some verses copied onto a blank leaf," they comment that "it lacks poetic diction, and the meter is not according to classical standards, but is has certain forcefulness in its imagery."[23] Since it cannot lack poetic diction, being poetic, and since "classical standards" were long past in the Old English tradition, there is no reason why it should be measured by an irrelevant and presentist standard. It is also not a fragment, if by that is intended something unfinished or a text that is only a part of something larger. Instead, what we have in *The Grave* is a forceful poem, both in its insistent metre and its depiction of a close-sided and closed dwelling for the conscious corpse. But its horror is countered by its tenderness and familiar images of a mother, of friends, and of emotive moments in *this* short life. The poet recognizes love and regrets its absence in the loss that death necessarily brings. Here, though, that loss is felt, impossibly, through the loneliness of the sentient dead.

For most scholars discussing the poem, the loss appears to be their own, because for them, this astonishing and moving poem is judged poorly for its *lack* of something: lack of novelty, lack of adherence to an earlier poetic tradition; its lack of completeness; its lack of complexity; its lack of originality. Scholars working in the twelfth and earlier thirteenth centuries on the hundreds of transformations of pre-Conquest exemplars, or on the numerous compositions that are themselves post-Conquest, are used to dealing with this idea of "lack." Such lacklustre reading has itself permitted the construction of a scholarly agenda that seems to highlight the existence of a perceived literary outlier like *The Grave* only to derogate it.

Decomposition

The Grave is a complete text in Bodley 343, consciously added to precisely fill the empty half of folio 170 recto in the manuscript (see figure 4 above).[24] *The Grave* is a third person address to a future corpse; that is, to all humanity and, in its compression on the page, the poem is visible at one glance—whole and entire. In measured and well-paced, elaborately detailed allit-

---

23 Fulk and Cain, *A History of Old English Literature*, 139 and 188.

24 The manuscript has been misfoliated in this quire—something not noted before. This foliation is seventeenth century, and folio "168" is missing. What is listed as folio 169 is actually 168; folio 170, upon which *The Grave* is written, is actually folio 169, the penultimate leaf of the quire of eight—quire 29. On the verso of fol. 170, and on fols. 171 and 172 are thirteenth-century Latin homilies and Alain de Lille's exposition of the sequence *Ad celebres rex celice*. See Conti and Da Rold, "Bodley 343," https://em1060.stanford.edu/manuscript/oxford-bodleian-library-bodley-343–2406.

erative verse, the authoritative voice reveals what the outcome of death will be: what the outcome has always been. This is no objective physiological account of decomposition, though the body's decay is very present. This poet wants to be sure the future-corpse understands the isolation, claustrophobia, and loveless situation of the grave: a precisely-fitting stone house in which one will live alone, time without end.[25]

It is a remarkable poem, and in my edited form using the common editorial practice of long alliterative verse lines it is twenty-five lines long.[26]

The Grave: An Edition

Đe wes bold ʒebyld | er þu iboren were;
ðe wes molde imynt | er ðu of moder come.
Ac hit nes no idiht, | ne þeo deopnes imeten;
nes ʒyt iloced | hu long hit þe were.
Nu me þe bringæð | þer ðu beon scealt.
Nu me sceæl þe meten | and þa molde seoððа.
Ne bið no þin hus | healice itinbred:
hit bið unheh and lah | þonne þu list þerinne;
ðe helewaʒes beoð laʒe, | sidwaʒes unheʒe,
þe rof bið ibyld | þire broste ful neh.
Swa ðu scealt on molde | wunien ful calde.
Dimme and deorcæ þet den | fulæt on honde.
Dureleas is þæt hus | and dearc hit is wiðinnen.
ðær þu bist feste bidytt | and dæð hefð þa cæʒe.
Ladlic is þæt eorð-hus | and grim inne to wunien.
ðer þu scealt wunien | and wurmes þe todeleð.
Đus ðu bist ileʒd | and ladæst þine fronden.
Nefst ðu nenne freond | þe þe wylle faren to,
ðæt efre wule lokien | hu þe þæt hus þe likie,
ðæt æfre undon | ðe wule ða dure
and þe æfter lihten.
For sone þu bist ladlic | and lad to iseonne.
For sone bið þin hæfet | faxes bireved,
al bið ðes faxes | feirnes forsceden;[27]
næle hit nan mit fingres | feire stracien.

25 Tombs and graves were sometimes built like small houses in pre-Conquest England. See Nilson, *Cathedral Shrines*, 34–35.

26 See Jones, "Re-lining *The Grave*," 71–75, for an alternative lineation and full metrical explanation. In this edition, the upright pipe represents a caesura in the middle of the long alliterative line.

27 Franzen, in an article denying these last three lines could be written by the

The Grave: A Translation[28]

For you a building was built before you were born;
For you an earthen grave was meant before you came from a mother;
But it was not prepared, nor its deepness measured;
nor was it yet ordained how long it might be for you.
Now someone will bring you to where you shall be;
now someone will measure you and the earth after that.
Nor is your house constructed highly:
it is unhigh and low when you lie in it;
the endwalls are low, the sidewalls unhigh,
the roof is built very close to your breast.
So you shall in earth live fully cold,
dim and dark that den grows foul at hand.
Doorless is that house and dark it is within;
there you are fast enclosed and death holds the key.
Loathsome is that earth-house and grim to live in;
there you will live and worms shall share you out.
Thus you will be laid and be most hateful to your friends.
You have no friend who will come to you,
who will ever find out how that house suits you,
who will ever undo the door for you
...and come in after you.
For soon you are loathly and hateful to see:
for soon your head will lose its hair,
all the hair's fairness will be shed;
no one with their fingers will gently stroke it.

The Grave is, then, an English alliterative poem datable to ca. 1180–1200, belonging to a much longer tradition of works in that form. It is written as a later addition onto the blank lines of fol. 170r by scribes who are seen elsewhere in Bodley 343. The poem should be considered an integral part of Bodley 343's homiletic impulse, executed in two stages by the poem's scribes to round off the codex, but in a manner that is deeply respectful of the original lay-out of the text within the prepared writing grid. In the hands of *The Grave*, palaeographical features that might individually add up to very little on their own, especially when the heterogeneous nature of contemporary script is considered, come together to add up to this re-dating for the poem, confirmed by other scribal examples that might be evaluated along-

Tremulous Hand of Worcester, also suggests editors have mistranscribed "forsceden" for "forpurden." This seems right to me. See her "On the Attribution of Additions," 8.

28 This is a quite literal translation, following, for the most part, the syntax—slightly awkward though it seems in modern English.

side it. The scribe of the first thirteen manuscript lines of *The Grave* in the bottom third of fol. 170r is very likely to be the same hand as that in the preceding many folios—the main scribe of Bodley 343. Although the poem is entered into the manuscript as an addition, probably some time after the final homiletic stint was finished on fol. 170r, enough features of the hand are shared to suggest the same scribe is at work. Some of the definitive features are the high, round-backed **d**, sometimes formed with two distinct strokes of the pen (one creating the back, the other the bowl); a high **f** with a rounded topstroke; a distinctive form of **g** that is written as if a **t** first, before the tail is added; an **h** with the first limb curved up on the line and the second swooping to the left below the line; and the two-shaped **r** in ligature. Features that indicate *The Grave* is a slightly later, and less formal manifestation of this same hand, include the less well-defined Tironian *nota*; and the absence of the otiose stroke embellishing the tail of **g**.

Overall, characteristics of letter forms in French and Latin manuscripts that can be used to assist in dating English manuscripts like Bodley 343 in the later twelfth century include (arranged chronologically here from the second part of the twelfth century to the end of the century): a closed-tail **g** from the middle of the twelfth century; the bow at the top of **a** closes upon the lower part of the letter; there are straight(ish) abbreviation marks; descenders which swing to the left; and straight, exaggerated ascenders are penned on the top line. *Litterae elongatae* or elongated and elaborated letters appear in the second half of the century, perhaps influenced by papal documents. From the third quarter of the twelfth century, onset or first letter strokes become lozenge shaped; the Tironian *nota* sits on the ruled line not below it; and "biting" **p** occurs (in literary documents). After ca. 1170, straight lines, angles and shallow curves take the place of full curves in the letters **a**, **b**, **c**, **d**, **e**, **g**, **m**, **n**, **o**, **t**; the **d+e** ligature appears; trailing-headed **a** appears; the cross-stroke of **t** turns downward; and the horizontal feet of minims become more pronounced. Towards the very end of the twelfth century, as seen in Bodley 343, ruling patterns change, most notably with the extension of the three middle lines of writing grid into both margins; loss of **e**-*caudata*; both Caroline and long **r** are used; hairlines appear at the bottom of round **r**; the right limb of **h** begins to extend below the line; and the 9-shaped abbreviation for *con-* comes into use.[29]

29 Ker, *English Manuscripts*, 37–38; Derolez, *The Palaeography of Gothic*, 62–67 and plate 13. Parkes, *English Cursive Book Hands*; Wright, *English Vernacular*. The dating system used here is typical: "s." indicates "*saeculum*" (century); "xii" indicates twelfth; "med" indicates "middle"; "ex" indicates "the end of"; and more precision is obtained through the use of quarter-centuries. The suprascript "2" indicates "second-half of."

These dating features in French and Latin are illustrated in writing in English, even if only in Latin words or phrases within the English. The particularity of working with English texts, as opposed to both French and Latin,[30] primarily centres on the aspect (the general look of the hand) and, less so, on the *ductus* (the number, direction, and angle of the pen-strokes) of English: the aspect of English is obviously denser and more vertical by virtue of the greater number of ascenders and descenders. In relation to *ductus*, the resulting differences in weight and chiaroscuro (or light and shade) are significant: English texts are often written with a less broad nib and with greater cursivity. English, in the twelfth and thirteenth centuries, is rarely used within *de luxe* volumes where one finds the most formal of scripts, unless it so happens that a verse in English is contained within the predominantly Latin narrative, as is the case with *Bede's Death-Song* in Oxford, Bodleian Library, Digby 11, fol. 108r.[31] There the script of the English is essentially similar to the regular Gothic *textura rotunda* seen in the Latin. Perhaps most significantly, the analysis shows that the copying of *The Grave* in Bodley 343 is an approximately contemporaneous addition—within a decade or two of the completion of the homilies up to fol. 170r—one that as I argue was completed partly by the main scribe of the manuscript, whose hand, as Wilcox and others are clear, transforms as the various parts of the homiliary were produced.[32]

Not only are elements of the hand of the final lines of *The Grave* congruent with that of the main scribe, but the codicological fit is highly significant. The initial writer of *The Grave* sought principally to squeeze the poem into the available space at lines 29–43 of fol. 170r. This left very little room at the bottom of the folio. When a slightly later scribe, writing perhaps early in the thirteenth century, decided to come back and round off the poem with the personal touch about the stroking of one's hair, the final lines had to be entered, somewhat untidily, and with significant compression. This is sur-

30 On which, see Denholm-Young, *Handwriting*, 36, who erroneously comments that English was never written like Latin or Anglo-Norman. English was often, but not always, more cursive and "informal" than Latin.

31 See Derolez, *Palaeography*, 69–70, for the arguments about the emergence of proto-gothic and Gothic in England, perhaps as a result of the influence of English Vernacular Minuscule or insular script. It seems that English, on many occasions, diverges from the Latin, which is curious. Did those writing the vernacular always seek to make it different? The later development of Anglicana in the thirteenth century suggests so. I owe the reference to Digby 11 to Matthew Aiello.

32 Wilcox, "Oxford, Bodleian Library, Bodley 343," in his *Homilies by Ælfric*, 71–101; Irvine, *Old English Homilies*.

prising given that the entire verso of fol. 170 would have still been blank at this point. It seems that above all the scribe or scribes wanted to maintain the textual integrity of *The Grave* on the recto of the folio.

What would have driven the scribes to be so insistent on maintaining the visual integrity of the folio, squeezing in the text like this, and breaking out of the writing grid? For the scribes of Bodley 343 and their spatial perspective, textual integrity was part of the motivation in the manuscript's compilation, and this is how the manuscript was put together.[33] In other words, in terms of textual aesthetic, *The Grave* is a carefully thought-through addition responding to the specific manuscript context, not some random or fragmentary poem. The scribes carefully followed the line-length provided by the original ruling for the writing grid, respecting the simple *mise-en-page*, though extending the number of lines. The poem—as is the case with all earlier Old English poetry—has no title and is written in long lines across the folio. Only the white space left blank after the preceding double *positurae* (heavy punctuation marks that look like a semi-colon but with two dots) and the scribal transition lets the reader know this is a new text.

The poem is thematically linked to the immediately preceding homily, demonstrating that *The Grave*'s scribes knew the contents of the English texts in this part of Bodley 343. The preceding prose piece is Ælfric's second Homily for a Confessor (Assmann iv), which explicates the pericope Matthew 24:42–47; that is, be vigilant and ready for death because one does not know when Christ will come.[34] At lines 95–98 in the edited text, the Old English homily reveals:

> Ðæs hiredes ealdor soðlice is urea gen mod, and se dyrna þeof, þe digollice cymð, is se gemænelica deaþ, ðe þæs mannes lichaman mid his digelan tocyme to deaðe gebringað.
>
> The master of the household is our own spirit and the hidden thief who comes secretly is universal death who, with his secret arrival, carries the man's body off to death.

It is not difficult to see how a reader of that homily would be inspired to include *The Grave* as the fitting, final piece in the manuscript, despite its probably not being part of the original compiler's plan of texts. The poem, replete with complex rhetorical patternings and devices so well brought out by Douglas Short some thirty-five years ago is a masterpiece by anyone's

33 As Conti pointed out, though he did not discuss *The Grave*; Conti, "Preaching Scripture and Apocrypha," 53–57.

34 Assmann, *Angelsächsische Homilien*.

standards.[35] Its aesthetic appeal captures poets' imaginations: Longfellow translated it, albeit rather loosely; Borges translated it into a highly assonant and evocative modern Spanish version; and Edwin Morgan rendered it into a modern poetic version in two stanzas.[36]

For this scribe-author, the poem represents more than something clichéd or trite, or simply part of a tradition. This poet, perhaps inspired by homilies on death, provides a rather personal account of a universal inevitability, indirectly exhorting the audience to make the very most of *this* life, without—as homilists tend to do—comparing the vicissitudes of earthly existence with the eternal horrors or joys of the Christian afterlife. This poem is entirely about this life in a cycle that moves deterministically from pre-birth to post-death; from an inexistence to a dissolution; but always from an individual perspective, even as the entire human race is indicated by the second-person singular pronoun "þu," and its variant forms, used repetitively and pointedly throughout the twenty-five long alliterating lines. As the recipient of the troubling words of the somewhat aloof and apparently omniscient poet, the solitary person—"you"—becomes isolated, seemingly lacking community in this depiction of both birth and death. The unconsciousness of the pre-birth existence depicted in the first two lines, with an unspoken expectation that the unborn will find a welcome, is in profound contrast to the posthumous consciousness that the corpse will experience within the foul and dark grave. The being-in-the-grave will face an isolation that is the worse because of the lived knowledge of community, of family and friends that are an anticipated part of life; all these companions, with their attendant tenderness and love, choose to absent themselves from the new deathly home of the poet's "you."

The solitariness of the grave, the poet stresses, is forever; in lines 19 and 20, the friends of the being-in-the-grave will never come to visit, never step through the door. This contrasts with the transience of becoming alive, stressed by the phrasal repetition of "er ðu," "before you," in the opening lines. The poem opens, then, with the being-in-the-grave on the threshold of life; it closes with the being on the threshold of death, emphasized by the adverbial phrase, repeated at the start of lines 23 and 24, "for sone," "soon." Death for this "you" is imminent, as is it for all sentient beings; it is preordained; it pre-exists life.

35 Short, "Aesthetics and Unpleasantness"; and now, especially, Jones, "Relining *The Grave*."

36 Longfellow, *Poems*, 697–98; Borges and Kodama, *Breve Antología Anglosajona*; and Morgan, "The Grave," from *Dies Irae*, 39–40, re-published in *Poems of Thirty Years*.

The knowingness of the poet is matter of fact with not only no room for the being-in-the-grave to move within the earthen dwelling, but also no room for negotiation. The darkness of posthumous existence is dramatically symbolized by the definitive stepping sound of <d> in the three-line alliterative incremental stresses at lines 12–14: "dimme," "deorcaæ," "dureleas," "dæð." Here, too, this is a personified Death who, unlike St. Peter with the keys to heaven, has the key to the paradoxically doorless house of death; this is an earth-house with no exit.[37] The spotlight on the inescapability of death, rather than effecting a sense of *contemptus mundi* to focus the Christian's eyes heavenward, concentrates the mind on the corporeal: the length and breadth of the carefully measured, body-hugging grave; the claustrophobic low and unhigh walls grasping the body; the chill and blackness of the interior; the gradual decomposition of the foul body, eaten by worms, close at hand; and finally other parts of the body themselves becoming "hateful to look upon." The closing three lines, added by a shaky hand finding it difficult to write at the very bottom of the folio, zoom in on the detail of the corpse's hair. The scribe that wrote these few lines as a response to "For sone þu bist ladlic and lad to iseonne" ("For soon you are loathsome and hateful to see") at line 22—

> For sone bið þin hæfet | faxes bireved,
> al bið ðes faxes | feirnes forsceden;
> næle hit nan mit fingres | feire stracien.
>
> for soon your head will lose its hair,
> all the hair's fairness will be shed;
> no one with their fingers will gently stroke it.

encourages contemplation not only of physical decay, but also of the futility of vanity. As will be seen in Chapter 4, the scribe is identical to a hand that corrects the main text, and that enters a liturgical text on the Virgin Mary with neumes and insular-style clefs at folio x recto of Bodley 343, datable to the very beginning of the thirteenth century. The emphasis on devotion to the Virgin Mary is part of a wider movement of veneration and liturgical celebration of the saint by twelfth- and thirteenth-century monks, but also by nuns.[38]

---

37 *Dureleas* only otherwise occurs in the *Worcester Fragments*, poems copied or written by the Tremulous Hand of Worcester in a manuscript also containing Ælfric's *Grammar* and *Glossary*. See Moffat, *The Soul's Address to the Body*. In an interesting real-life parallel, some medieval anchoresses entered into anchorholds the doors of which were then bricked up, so that only contact through a small window was possible.

38 Other music for Marian worship, and a note on the Virgin's age, are added to the

Here, in *The Grave*, by highlighting the perishing fair hair (perhaps white hair of old age, or blonde hair, or simply beautiful hair), the poet captures an image of an audience concerned with how they look—and, albeit stereotypically, this may suggest an intended female audience. In particular, the final line captures an intimate moment of hair being stroked, as if this were the present living delight of the soon-to-be dead person. The personal depiction of gentle hair-stroking casts us back to birth at the beginning of the poem—a mother and her baby; or to loving friends and companions at lines 17–18 who *do* visit during this life, who do care; but who will find the subject hateful and will no longer visit after death.

The Grave offers a series of dramatic contrasts between life and death that are not explicitly linked to God, a Christian community, or an eternal afterlife, other than as being-in-the-grave. It focuses on *this* life—on the body, the physical structure of the earth-house. The senses are heightened: the "you" of the addressee is required to see the decaying body, which is their own future body; to touch the walls of the grave and feel the cold of the body's cessation; to hear the silence and isolation of the post-death enclosure of the grave; to smell and taste the decomposing body. As participants in a future death—which we all are—the poem seeks emotional engagement and individualizes the exhortation to watch out for death, which can come at any time.

Through contrasts, the physical process of death is detailed, together with the site of the body: the low end-walls, the unhigh side-walls; the company of friends, the isolation; the beauty of living, the horror of the house-like grave. The poem seems a fitting end-note to the manuscript that warns and exhorts a general audience, for here, at fol. 170r, the addressee is the single "you:" the individual, perhaps female, who knows the closeness of a loved one's gentle caress.[39] Phenomenologically, the closing of the manuscript called for the scribe's response, carefully measured to fit into the tight space of the half-blank folio. Emotionally, the poet may seem without hope: as grim and dark-minded as the grave itself. And yet, there is an implicit hope.

---

manuscript, too, at fols. x verso, 64v, and 154v, respectively. See *English Manuscripts 1060 to 1220*, "Bodley 343," by Conti and Da Rold. For the broader liturgical context of this text, see Ihnat, "Early Evidence for the Cult of Anne in Twelfth-Century England," especially 1–15, who stresses Worcester Benedictine Cathedral—dedicated to the Virgin Mary—as an dedicated centre of Marian devotion (like many other institutions). On Bodley 343's role in a broader institutional context, see Conti, "Individual practice."

39 Though subsequently, another scribe later added the Latin texts to fols. 170v–172v.

As Charles Wright suggested, it is likely that the poet of *The Grave* used the Old English text known as Vercelli Homily IX as a source (itself potentially influenced by the earlier Irish-Latin work, *Catechesis Celtica*).[40] *The Grave* and the Old English sermon known as Vercelli Homily IX share the literary topoi of the corpse shedding hair and the grave as a house, both images reappearing in the slightly later *Worcester Fragments*, written by the Tremulous Hand. *The Grave* thus becomes a nexus in a catena of literary transmission. To these sources can be added a broader structural influence for *The Grave*, with its focus on the individual spot identified for someone's burial, and the poem's tripartite framework of birth, death, and burial. It is emphatically and—in English literature up to this point, uniquely—reminiscent of, if not directly influenced by, the "Three Sods" proverbial tradition seen in the Irish *Lives of Madog* and, as follows, of Colum Cille:

> Acus bid a fhis agaib...go bfuilid tri foide and nach edir do aennech asechna .i. fód a gheine 7 fod a bais 7 fód a adhnacail. Acus adubairt an rann-sa:
>
> Tri fodain nach sechantar,
> mar aderid a mor-fhocuil:
> fód a gene, fód a bais,
> 7 fod a adhnacail.
>
> And wit ye well...there be three sods that none may escape, the sod of his birth and the sod of his death and the sod of his burying. And he spake this quatrain:
>
> Three little sods that cannot be shunned,
> As they say in the proverb;
> The sod of his birth and the sod of his death,
> And the sod of his burying.[41]

As Madoc explains in his *Life*: "The spot in which God has granted me to make last resting-place and above, that spot I will not forsake...for the sod on

40 Wright, *The Irish Tradition*, 95–100, where he suggests the influence on Vercelli Homily IX comes from the *Catechesis Celtica*, "Five Visions of Hell"; see also, Siebert, "A Possible Source for the Addition to *The Grave*," who attributes the reference to fingers caressing hair as being derived from debate literature in London, British Library, Royal MS 7 A. iii.

41 Plummer, "Life of Maedoc of Ferns," 229, § 159. This saint's life is rich with the significance of place. The text and translation is from O'Kelleher and Schoepperle, *Betha Colaim Chille*, 102 (http://archive.org/details/bethacolaimchill00odonuoft) and Lacey, *Manus O'Donnell's Life of Colum Cille*. I am grateful to Dr. Anne Marie D'Arcy for suggesting these Irish texts to me.

which I stand is the sod of my resurrection and burial."[42] Thus, in *The Grave*, what *appears* to be a text about the transience of life and the inevitability of death and decay is also, unequivocally (and in back-reference to Ælfric's homily preceding it in Bodley 343) actually about resurrection at Judgement Day: the individual's predestined place, their sod, their "bold" ("building") from which they are preordained to rise. The poem thus belongs in the devotional and contemplative tradition, with a hopeful eschatological tone, not the poem as G. K. Anderson read it: "Grim, macabre, but vivid and unforgettable; the quintessence of the elegiac; the essence of the terror of death, but with no Judgement Day to break the spell: sans wine, sans singer, and sans end." I would argue, on the contrary, that the Three Sods motif employed here absolutely suggests the hope and company of the resurrected soul for those whose education gave them access to this knowledge.[43]

The striking reference to the perishing of the being-in-the-grave's hair is also, potentially, an allusion to resurrection and the hope of an eternal afterlife in joy, rather than the dim, dark grave. Luke 21:16–19 reminds the Christian that at the end of times: "[Y]ou shall be betrayed by your parents and brethren, and kinsmen and friends; and some of you they will put to death [17] And you will be hated by all men for my name's sake. [18] But a hair of your head shall not perish. [19] In your patience you shall possess your souls." This promise of blissful resurrection (despite the physical hair perishing in the grave) would be familiar to those steeped in the Gospels who heard or read *The Grave*, which functions through contrast between this physical world and an implied spiritual existence.[44] Conybeare claimed this poem was a fragment spoken by death, and printed it as such, ending

---

42 See Plummer, *Bethada Náem nÉrenn*, 2:229. This *Life* also has a twelfth-century Welsh reflex, extant in London, British Library, Cotton MS Vespasian A. xiv, fols. 96v–104v, a manuscript possibly produced in Wales in the twelfth and earlier thirteenth century. Interestingly for *The Grave*, in the *Life of Maedoc*, a "churl" sees "a number of young and distinguished monks with fair golden hair" (Plummer, *Bethada Náem nÉrenn*, 2:230–31).

43 Anderson, *The Literature of the Anglo-Saxons*, 189. See also Ó hÓgáin, "Migratory Legends," 67ff. I owe this latter reference to Dr. Anne Marie D'Arcy.

44 The only other similar phrase is "Þet an her of hare fax ne schulde forwurðen," spoken of St. Katherine and recorded by the *Middle English Dictionary* (s.v. fax, meaning specifically "hair of the head") as occurring in the West Midlands manuscript, London, British Library, Royal MS 17. A. xxvii, dated to ca. 1225, and containing texts from the Katherine-Group and Wooing Group, probably designed for a female religious readership. On this manuscript generally, see Kim, "Female Readers."

his edition at line 22.[45] Clearly Bodley 343's scribe of the last three lines was inspired to add the final thoughts that I have read as offering hope. He or indeed *she* was motivated to continue the conversation about death—everyone's death—in the full knowledge of the lines that preceded the later addition.

Detailed reading of a short poem like *The Grave* reveals it to be a rich, profound commentary on all things—past, present, future. It is no wonder this moving and disturbing poem attracted the attention of Borges and of Edwin Morgan and others. Being alert to the resonance of *The Grave* means being alive to the dynamic textual production that scholars need to cultivate in the consideration of small texts, "bits" of texts, marginalia and so-called "fragments." In its origin, or in its received form, *The Grave* is not a fragment; it is a complete account of a predestined human life, where the person's existence is known before they are born. For the reader, reflecting on this poem and its depiction of a conscious death, *The Grave* might certainly be intended to make one stronger in heart and sounder of intent as such devotional and educative poetry intends to do. It represents the finest short work in English of the period—a time considered by some, as discussed in Chapter 2, to represent the nadir of English. The poem is an ironic self-death, then, though as I have suggested it might instead be regarded as offering textual hope: that in the closing of Bodley 343 the scribe(s) knew perfectly well that their vernacular was far from dead and buried, and their addition of *The Grave* provides firm evidence for this.[46]

---

45 Conybeare, *Six Articles*, 1–5, reprinted in Conybeare, ed., *Illustrations of Anglo-Saxon Poetry*, 270–73, as a "Norman-Saxon Fragment on Death."

46 As well as his translation, and as discussed above in Chapter 1, Borges also wrote two haiku (Borges, *La cifra*). The haikus read: "El hombre ha muerto. / La barba no lo sabe. / Crecen las uñas." ("A man lies dead; / yet his nails, beard and hair / continue to grow, unaware.") And "Esta es la mano / que alguna vez tocaba / tu cabellera." This is translated by Brighid Hanlon-Baker, in a private communication, as "This is the hand / that once touched / your hair." Hair and its continuing growth or its loss after death unite *The Grave* here and the *Letter of Eadwine* in Chapter 1.

Chapter 4

MANUSCRIPT AND SCRIPT

TIME AND PLACE

BOOK HISTORY AND diplomatic studies are areas of research into the written record that are usually treated and discussed separately and practised in hyper-specialist ways. This chapter will address the production of manuscript books and documents through the later eleventh to the first half of the thirteenth centuries to think across descriptive and analytical categories commonly in use in manuscript studies. Oxford, Bodleian Library, MS Bodley 343—the focus of Chapter 3 from a textual perspective—here provides the opening inspiration for a discussion of script and its changing nature, modern categorization, and dateability. This will include a re-dating of the writing of the Tremulous Hand of Worcester.

Medieval material objects provide evidence for hundreds of scribes writing on behalf of their religious institutions or as participants in coteries of writers and intellectuals. In these objects it is possible to see a full range of scribal practices—from what traditional palaeographers regard as the highest-grade Gothic book hand to scribes at the vanguard of contemporary trends in writing to those whose scripts could function across textual form. These written objects throw into sharp relief the tendencies of twentieth- and twenty-first-century scholars to utilize categories and hierarchies of scripts that are not reflected in the medieval materials themselves. The categories narrow the range of written records readily understood to be worthwhile studying from an aesthetic perspective. The manuscripts, rolls, and documents I discuss inspire my broader analysis of the modes and methods of writings in this crucially important period. Between ca. 1170 and 1230, especially, scripts and book production practices were in a vibrant and dynamic period of innovation and possibility of expression that cannot easily be categorized and might helpfully not be hierarchized.

As the last chapter showed, sometime in the late twelfth century, a scribe—whom few would consider calligraphically accomplished—added a poem to Oxford, Bodleian Library, MS Bodley 343, an extensive bilingual homiliary. At the time of their writing, this English lyric filled the last lines of the recto of the folio, and in so doing, completed the manuscript at that moment. For this scribe, it was important to round off the page, to offer final thoughts on this book and this world, and thus to have the last word, reminding readers how horrific is the death that awaits us all. The lines from

"7 grim inne to wunien" to the end of poem run on below the extent of the manuscript compiler's initially ruled writing grid:

> 7 grim inne to wunien. Ðer þu scealt wunien 7 wurmes þe todeleð. Ðus ðu
> bist ileȝd. 7 ladæst þine fronden. Nefst ðu nenne freond. þe þe wylle
> faren to. Ðæt efre wule lokien. hu þe þæt hus þe likie. Ðæt æfre undon.
> ðe wule ða dure. 7 þe æfter lihten. For sone þu bist ladlic 7 lad to iseonne.
>
> Loathsome is that earth-house and grim to live in. There you will live and worms shall share you out. Like this you will be laid and be most hateful to your friends. You will not have any friend who will come to you, who will ever find out how that house suits you, who will ever undo the door for you and come in after you. For soon you are loathly and hateful to see.

Judging by the features of the writing, at the beginning of the thirteenth century, after this English poem had been written out, another scribe added Latin texts to folios 170 verso and 171, and on an added folio 172. These include an excerpt from Alain de Lille's *Expositio prosae de angelis*, an early instance of the genre of sequence commentary that suggests the codex comprised principally of homilies was now becoming a contemporary reference volume for liturgical exposition.[1] Because of the desire to keep the English poetic text together visually, there was only the most marginal space for expansion when a scribe decided to *really* finish off *The Grave* with one and half lines of touching observation, as discussed in Chapter 3 above:

> for sone bið þin hæfet. faxes bireued. al bið ðes faxes feirnes forsceden.
> næle hit nan mit fingres feire stracien.
>
> for soon your head will lose its hair, all the hair's fairness will be shed;
> no one with their fingers will gently stroke it.

Beyond what the poem means, its alliterative scheme, personification of death, and claustrophobia of the permanent consciousness of having died—beyond this: who might have written this poem? What was the context in which it was created? How does the poem relate to the physical book through which it is made permanent? These questions matter for all kinds of reasons; they may be of most significance for literary scholars—especially those who recognize the continuity of the dynamic English tradition from the pre-Conquest into the high Middle Ages that is demonstrated by the case

---

1 See Kihlman, *Expositiones sequentiarum*, 7–8, where Bodley 343, as *Ox4*, described erroneously as a "thirteenth-century manuscript." See also Kihlman, "Medieval Sequence Commentaries." Bodley 343's text has particular readings in common with Oxford, Bodleian Library, MS Auct F. 6. 8 of the later thirteenth century with Gloucester connections.

studies in this present volume. But more, and to be investigated in this final chapter, these questions about the *spaces* and *practices* of textual production have important implications for advancing scholarly understanding of communities of training and the sociology of cultures of literacy, particularly in this period (the twelfth, or "long" twelfth century) which has so often been seen as "falling between" periods or a "movement towards" the completion of transition. This chapter will ask the fundamental questions of when, where, why, and by whom the marginal additions in Bodley 343 were written to open up the interpretative potential and interest of this manuscript and other contemporary written materials. This work challenges received wisdom in palaeography and manuscript studies that operates principally through types of script and hierarchies of textual production.

Scribal Practices and Bodley 343

The script of the initial verses of *The Grave* in Bodley 343 is written by the main scribe of the manuscript, whose hand is seen at folios 1–170 recto. This scribe was working in around 1180–1200. *The Grave* scribe's lines round off the recto and ensure the retention of a visual cogency to the manuscript—not taking the poem over to the verso. This is typical, as Aidan Conti's foundational research on this manuscript has shown; such attention to space is also evident in the original design of the manuscript.[2] It is also a feature, more generally, that typifies manuscript production in the post-1140 period: a desire to round off, to close up white space within the writing grid. This includes the regular provision of line-filler ornamentation and the lateral expansion of particular graphs like **N** or **S** to make sure the line ends tidily again the right edge of the writing grid, a phenomenon we would call "right justified" in the production of printed text.

Some years after this scribal effort, as established in Chapter 3, another scribe (different to *The Grave*'s main scribe, but responsible for other later additions to the manuscript) finished *The Grave* with words that touch on the hope of the resurrection. The hand of these final lines can be dated perhaps as much as a couple of decades after the writing of the first version of *The Grave*. Was the short addition effectively completing an already-existing and known poem? Were these new closing lines created afresh for this space? There is no doubt that the earlier lines of *The Grave* existed in an exemplar; evidence for this is provided by the erasures of the scribe's dittographic errors where they repeat "ȝe" at line 1, "hus" at line 4 of the poem,

2 Conti, "Preaching Scripture and Apocrypha."

and "7 dæð hefð" at line 9. But these three new verse-lines written over a manuscript line-and-a-half seem like a personal and meaningful intervention of a poet invested in dramatically highlighting the emotional connection between poem and reader that is present throughout the text.

It is likely that the second poet of fol. 170r was promulgating current spiritual thinking, and, I would speculate, devotional practices that make room for an individual's contemplation, especially in relation to women and women's lives of piety. This speculation gains credibility through analysis of the additional evidence provided by this same scribe, who filled other blank spaces in the manuscript with contemporary and innovative hymns and notes about the Virgin Mary.[3] The hand is idiosyncratic and includes notable features such as an angular upward rising cross stroke of high **f** and **s;** a Caroline form of **h** where the second limb extends below the line; a long **r;** an eth where the cross-stroke extends through the ascender and curves up at the right upper end. Comparison between these other additions at fol. x recto and at fol. 154v show this certainly to be the same hand as the closing poet of *The Grave.*

The sequence *Salve sanctarum sanctissima*, occurring at fol. x recto in Bodley 343, follows an incomplete Ælfrician homily for the sixteenth Sunday after Pentecost, and fills the remaining two thirds of the blank singleton (while another musical sequence fills the verso in a different hand). This music, comprised of a four-line stave and fully diastemmatic notation with C and F clef, especially at this date around the turn of the thirteenth century, makes these additions significant.[4] They confirm the use of the volume for those readers or browsers researching and contemplating liturgical formulations. An additional note detailing the age of the Virgin Mary at the time of Christ's birth is written in the same hand as the Marian musical sequences. This note occurs at fol. 154v on three of the five blank lines at the bottom of the ruled writing grid:

> [S]ancta Maria wes ðreo 7 sixti winter ða heo of middenærde ferde. 7 heo wes fiftene æld ða heo Crist acende. 7 heo wes mid him ðreo 7 ðritti winter on middenærde. 7 heo wes efter him sixtene gær on ðissere worlde.

> Saint Mary was sixty-three winters when she departed from this middle-earth. And she was fifteen years old when she gave birth to Christ. And she was with him for thirty-three winters on middle-earth. And she was in this world for sixteen years after him.

---

3 Ramsay came first to this conclusion in "A Possible 'Tremulous Hand' Addition."

4 Thanks to Benjamin Albritton for this description. See *The Sources of British Songs* project: https://www.diamm.ac.uk/documents/111/Salve-mater-salvatoris-mater-salutifera.pdf.

The music, the wisdom text, and the poetry change the function of the codex; it is augmented from its homiletic origins as a preaching book (as Conti suggests in contrast to Susan Irvine's categorization of the manuscript as "devotional"[5]) to an anthology of reference materials for worship and perhaps pastoral care. More, though, this scribe's additions refocus the manuscript towards not just the liturgical and the performative, but also to the Marian. Considering the addition of *The Grave*, with its final focus on the absence of gentle stroking of one's hair, as well as the composition of specifically Marian sequences and microtexts, it is worth asking whether women might have owned the manuscript at this period shortly after its initial production.

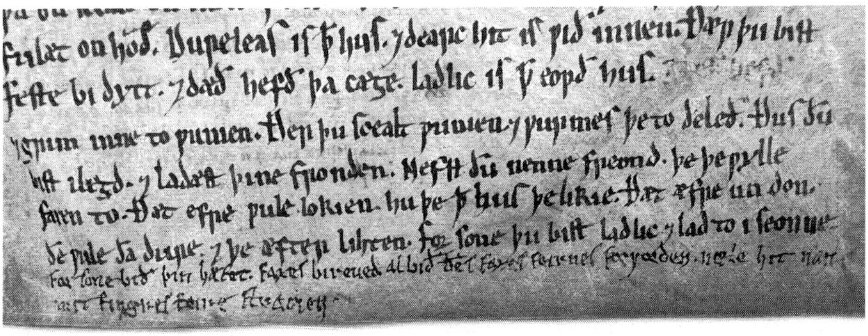

Figure 5. Oxford, Bodleian Library, Bodley MS 343, fol. 170r (detail). Photograph by the author. © The Bodleian Library, Oxford.

Dating Script and the Tremulous Hand

The last three verses of *The Grave* are written as one-and-a-half long lines at the very bottom of fol. 170r of Bodley 343 (Fig. 5). These lines have attracted some scholarly attention because they exhibit a tremor and are therefore reminiscent of the Tremulous Hand. The Tremulous Hand, or Tremulous Scribe, was a religious figure working somewhere in the West Midlands in the later twelfth and earlier thirteenth centuries. They are usually placed at Worcester, though they might have used the library at Worcester Priory without being resident at that Benedictine institution. The Tremulous Hand wrote English poetry, compiled a version of Ælfric's *Glossary*, and annotated, punctuated, and modernized many Old English manuscripts linked with Worcester in this post-Conquest period using both Latin and English in these processes.

5 Conti, "Preaching Scripture and Apocrypha."

In 2006, the Tremulous Hand scholar and editor, Christine Franzen, disputed the possibility that the verse, the music, and the note about the age of the Virgin Mary in Bodley 343 were by the famous Tremulous Hand.[6] This is an issue worth revisiting, however. As the place of origin of Bodley 343 is not assured, an identification of the Tremulous Hand would provide critical information about the possible localization and provenance of the manuscript. They were certainly active around 1200, when these Marian additions were made.

The Tremulous Hand of Worcester has been the focus of outstanding scholarship in recent decades.[7] This prolific reader and writer is likely to have been researching and composing religious and scholarly works in the West Midlands, with access to manuscript collections at extensive monastic libraries, like that at Worcester Cathedral priory. The scribe's numerous annotations, glosses, and reflections in English and in Latin, as well as their own poetic compositions, are contained in numerous extant volumes, including the Early English books, now Oxford, Bodleian Library, MSS Hatton 113, 114, 115, and 116, and Worcester Cathedral Library, MS F. 174.[8] This figure's importance has been rendered *outré* both by scholars who want to see the ongoing continuity of the pre-Conquest literary tradition and by those who would see in the Tremulous Hand the last vestiges of the understanding of Old English, but the reading and annotating of earlier manuscripts was not uncommon in the twelfth and thirteenth centuries.[9] This scholar's *oeuvre* seems to extend over decades, and their work is examined in detail by Christine Franzen, who detects many layers of effort over many years. While it was thought that the temporal progress of the scribe's writing, manifested through the noticeable tremor in their hand, was due to a degenerative disease, though, recent research has suggested the shakiness might *not* be an indicator of a progressive illness. This has important implications for the timeframe in which this scribe might have been working.[10]

Scholars have relied on the assessment of the great palaeographer, Neil R. Ker, to date the Tremulous Scribe's career. In a widely cited article, Ker

---

6 Franzen, "On the Attribution of Additions."

7 On this scribe, see Franzen, *The Tremulous Hand of Worcester*; Collier, "The Tremulous Worcester Hand"; Franzen, "The Tremulous Hand of Worcester and the Nero Scribe"; and Johnson, "The Micro-Texts of the Tremulous Hand."

8 On all of these, see Franzen, *Tremulous Hand*; and *The Production and Use of English.*

9 See, for example, Treharne, "Making their Presence Felt."

10 Thorpe and Alty, "What Type of Tremor Did the Medieval 'Tremulous Hand of Worcester' Have?"

suggested the Tremulous Scribe might have been writing and annotating as late as the middle of the thirteenth century.[11] This was surmised on the strength of evidence provided by one marginal addition in Oxford, Bodleian Library, MS Hatton 114, fol. 10r[12] (Fig. 6).

On this folio in Hatton 114, a thirteenth-century scribe entered a marginal table of contents written in a practised Gothic *textura rotunda* (a book hand, where the feet of the minims are rounded) in twenty-three very short lines in the outer margin. The Tremulous Scribe subsequently corrected this table of contents, and added glosses that, by their placement, clearly post-date the table of contents. In his cursory discussion, Ker's "evidence" is his inclination that the hand of the Table of Contents is dateable as late as the middle of the thirteenth quarter, but no palaeographical analysis is provided to support this. Ker states of the hand of the table of contents that it:

> Belongs, probably, to the second quarter of the thirteenth century; it can hardly be earlier than 1225 and may not be much, if at all, earlier than 1250.[13]

As confirmation of this dating to the second quarter of the thirteenth century, in a footnote, Ker thanks another palaeographer, Noel Denholm-Young, for permitting him "to quote his opinion that the hand is the middle of the thirteenth century."[14] The "middle of the thirteenth century" is not synonymous with the date of 1225–1250 that Ker supposes, so it is necessary to try to reconstruct what evidence might be being alluded to here. This probable palaeographical corroboration has to be extrapolated from the discussion of

---

11 Ker, "The Date of the 'Tremulous' Worcester Hand," Chapter 6, in *Books, Collectors and Libraries*, 67–69. This was first published as Ker as "The Date of the Tremulous Worcester Hands" in 1937.

12 The whole manuscript is digitized online, along with its companion volume, Oxford, Bodleian Library, MS Hatton 113. The current URL is https://digital.bodleian.ox.ac.uk/objects/e824c828-88be-48e7-8325-ebc22d542081/, accessed March 19, 2024.

13 Ker, "Date," 69.

14 Ker, "Date," 69. The significance of Ker's article is illustrated by subsequent scholarship's adoption of his dating. Collier, for example, in her "The Tremulous Worcester Scribe and his Milieu," 6, states: "Ideas about the tremulous hand were radically altered by Neil Ker's important article of 1937. Earlier commentators and editors almost unanimously dated the script to the later twelfth century. Ker demonstrated that the scribe was writing well into the thirteenth century, certainly around 1225, and perhaps as late as 1250, although he thought the duct of the script was formed in the late twelfth century. He arrived at this conclusion through an examination of a table of contents written in the margin of Bodleian MS Hatton 11[4]. The hand in which this table is written can be dated more or less definitely to the second quarter of the thirteenth century."

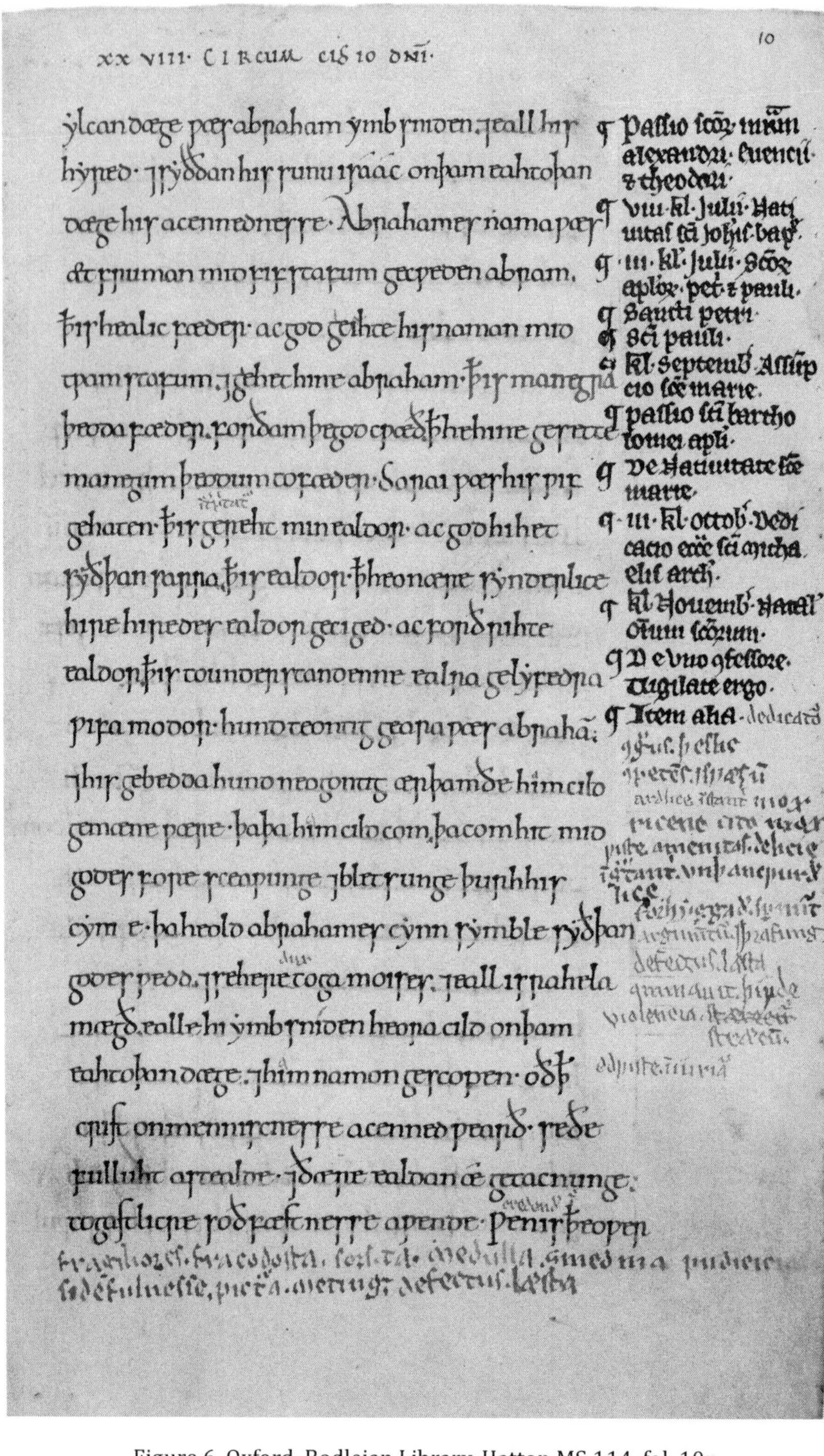

Figure 6. Oxford, Bodleian Library, Hatton MS 114, fol. 10r.

script in Denholm-Young's *Handwriting of England and Wales*.[15] There, the two most relevant features to be found for Denholm-Young's dating towards 1250 for the marginal addition in Hatton 114 seem to be the evolution of the enlarged head of **a** as that graph became double-compartment; and the emergence of the stem of **t** above the crossbar.[16] If it is these two features to which Denholm-Young pointed for dating the small marginal text, this is a tenuous argument indeed; in this table of contents, one double-compartment **a** occurs, and one instance of **t** with the stem rising above the crossbar. Other features *might* be the crossed downstroke of the Tironia *nota* and the barred capital **N** in "Nativitate" and "Novembris," though both of these palaeographical elements are common in writing that dates from the end of the twelfth century. With the **t** and the **a**, however, even in Denholm Young's *Handwriting in England and Wales*, his summary of dating features at the back of the book mitigates against using them as characteristics of mid-thirteenth-century script; there, he refers to the closing of the head of **a** as being ca. 1275 and the innovation of the form of **t** with a pierced cross-stroke as being around 1330–1350.

Further, to impressionistically date not only the Hatton 114 addition itself, but the *terminus* of the career of the Tremulous Scribe like this is a questionable process. Research focused on contemporary manuscripts and documents and the vast resources of digital manuscript repositories suggests that Ker's dating pushes the Tremulous Scribe's work too far into the thirteenth century. I would consider the scribe to be working no later than the first quarter of the thirteenth century, since dated and dateable examples of script from ca. 1180–ca. 1250 show that the features of the hand of the Tremulous Scribe are themselves dateable to the end of the twelfth and beginning of the thirteenth century.[17] The most extensive range of the hand exists in the fragmentary manuscript, Worcester Cathedral Library, MS F. 174, where the *ductus* is not a developed Gothic, and its graphic characteristics are most commonly found in hands dateable to about 1200.

A great deal hangs upon identifying the main features that would have led to the dating of this Table of Contents as middle of the thirteenth cen-

15 Denholm-Young, *Handwriting of England and Wales*.

16 Denholm-Young, *Handwriting of England and Wales*, 27: "In the second half of the [thirteenth] century the bow at the top of the a closes down (as in court hand) upon the lower part of the letter. About the same time it is common to find the vertical stroke of t piercing the cross-bar."

17 See, below, and see Prescott and Treharne, "The Origin and Context of the Salisbury Magna Carta" and Aiello, "English Vernacular Script," as well as standard palaeographical introductions.

tury or at least second quarter. The two-page article by Ker, with its footnote to Denholm Young's opinion, presents us with no measurable evidence for dating the career of the Tremulous Hand. It may be a superb and informed guess, but it is one that pushes the work of the Tremulous Hand to an unacceptably late date. These features—the form of **a** and the form of **t**—can be found earlier than the second quarter of the thirteenth century; and ca. 1225 is the *latest* point at which the Tremulous Hand would have been working. It is important to note that the script type and grade are significant here: the more formal and set the hand, the less graphically idiosyncratic. The Table of Contents shows some degree of formality and is, perhaps, the hand of a professional scribe in training. The scribe might feasibly have been in training under the Tremulous Hand, since Tremulous corrects the scribe's effort to list the contents of Hatton 114.

Evidence to suggest a latest date of around 1225 for this scribal work in the Table of Contents can be found in multiple manuscripts. In London, British Library, Cotton MS Claudius E. iii, fols. 3–168, for example, the form of **a** with a closed head is found in abundance, while **t** where the stem intersects the shaft, is found regularly.[18] In London, British Library, MS Harley 4751, a manuscript, possibly from Salisbury, containing a Bestiary with some additions from Gerald of Wales's *Topographia Hibernica* is written in an accomplished Gothic *Rotunda* that shows regular use of the bow of double-compartment **a** touching the lower bowl, and a very occasional slight protrusion of the shaft of **t** above the cross-stroke. It is dated to the late twelfth or early thirteenth centuries. In Pamela Robinson's *Dated and Datable Manuscripts in London Libraries*, examples of earlier thirteenth-century manuscripts that show the cross-stroke of **t** being pierced by the shaft and an almost complete closure of the bowl of **a** include London, Victoria and Albert Museum, MS L. 404–1916 from Lesnes between 1197 and 1230 (though probably written no later than 1220); London, Society of Antiquaries, MS 59, made in England between 1214 and 1222; and London, Lambeth Palace Library, MS 236, made between 1215 and 1223.[19] The first two manuscripts are liturgical and written in Gothic *textura precissa*, the most formal of the Gothic script-sys-

18 The manuscript, dated to 1197, is written in a Gothic *textura rotunda/precissa*. It contains *Abbreviationes Chronicorum* and *Ymagines Historiarum* by Ralph of Diceto. See the British Library's digital manuscript website, for fols. 119r and 125v of Cotton Claudius E. iii.

19 Robinson, *Catalogue of Dated and Datable Manuscripts*, plates 18, 21, and 22, respectively. Some images from the Lesnes Missal are available on the Victoria and Albert Museum website: https://collections.vam.ac.uk. See also London, British Library, Cotton MS Vitellius C. xii/2, which is dated to the first quarter of the

tem; the latter is written in a Gothic *textura rotunda*, the least formal of the four Gothic *textura* (or book hand) subdivisions. Contemporary examples of manuscripts that are yet more informal and more cursive include London, British Library, MS Sloane 1580 and London, British Library, Cotton MS Tiberius B. xiii. As less formal hands, with some features of charter hand (including the barred capitals and early Gothic *Anglicana* looped **d**) these are also more advanced in the inclusion of datable features such as the **a** and **t** under discussion. Both are dated to the first quarter of the thirteenth century.[20] Manuscripts with features parallel to those in Hatton 114's marginal Table of Contents are by no means exclusive to a post-1225 date of production, then. For arguably even greater relevance to the dating of the Tremulous Hand who seemed to work in or have access to the Worcester Cathedral Priory's books, London, British Library, Additional MS 89137, the "Descriptive Rental of Worcester Cathedral Priory," includes at fol. 80r a text dated to 1253.[21] Here, there is a considerably greater "modernness" of the script at *circa* 1250 that could be usefully compared with the Hatton 114 Table of Contents, if we are to follow Ker's and Denholm-Young's dating. To my eye, the Table of Contents in Hatton 114 *firmly* predates the localisable Worcester commentary hand in Additional MS 89137. This is to say, and let me be clear, the Table of Contents and thus the hand of the Tremulous Scribe are both decades earlier than Ker proposes.

By comparison, now the hand of the scribe who wrote the later lines of *The Grave* and the Marian texts in Oxford, Bodleian Library, Bodley MS 343, with whom this all began, can be seen to be contemporary with the Tremulous Scribe, and operating around the beginning of the thirteenth century.

From Time to Place

Oxford, Bodleian Library, Bodley MS 343 has been connected with Worcester, principally because many manuscripts written in English or containing glosses in the hand of the Tremulous Scribe were produced (and some still reside) at Worcester.[22] The appearance of a drawing of St. Wulfstan of Worcester is also evidence that the manuscript's localization can be attrib-

---

thirteenth century. Fol. 281r containing the *Life of Becket* has a **t** and an **a** in precisely the form that Ker would date as *middle* of the thirteenth century.

20 See the British Library digital manuscript website for images.

21 See London, British Library, Additional MS 89137 at the British Library digital manuscripts website.

22 See, for example, the discussion in Irvine, *Old English Homilies*; and Clemoes, *Ælfric's Catholic Homilies*.

uted to a place where that saint's cult was venerated. Bodley 343 has also been assigned to Worcester principally because it contains English written in the post-Conquest period, when relatively few centres of production seem to have been engaged in manufacturing vernacular texts. The copying of English was certainly maintained in the twelfth and earlier thirteenth centuries at institutions such as Worcester, Canterbury, Rochester, and, Peterborough. This knowledge, and the impulse to suggest origins at sites already known to produce manuscripts in English, has had the effect of proscribing other religious centres as places of manufacture for books and texts written in English.[23] *If* the scribe under discussion who wrote the end of *The Grave* and the Marian hymns is not the Tremulous Hand, then what else might prompt scholars to assert a Worcester connection for Bodley 343? More to the point, as others have commented, if it were a Worcester manuscript, then where is the Tremulous Hand within it? One might expect to see the scribe intervening in an English manuscript kept at the cathedral, as seems to have been the case with so many pre-Conquest and twelfth-century books.[24]

Other evidence might support a Worcester localization for Bodley 343. This connection takes the form of the strange image of a Bishop Wulfstan as an addition to the blank fol. 173r in Bodley 343. This has been tenuously dated to the thirteenth century,[25] but seems to be clearly later than that with its use of a distinctly *emulative*, and probably early modern, English Vernacular Minuscule reading "þ[a]n biscopen þan Wolstane god," complete with wynn and insular **g** that suggest the legend, and the image itself, were copied from something earlier. There are two potential Wulfstans, though the later is the more likely candidate: Wulfstan I was bishop of Worcester and archbishop of York, who died in 1023; and Wulfstan II was bishop of Worcester in the later eleventh century. Wulfstan I's most *familiar* connection, though, is neither with York nor with Worcester, but instead with Ely

23 On this, see Treharne, *Living through Conquest.*

24 Manuscripts written in, glossed by, and worked upon by the Tremulous Hand that have a Worcester localization, provenance, or connections include Cambridge, Corpus Christi College, MS 178; and Oxford, Bodleian Library, Hatton MSS 113, 114, 115, and 116, among others. See Franzen, *The Tremulous Hand*. Other evidence comes, perhaps, from the language of some of the homilies that has been shown by Irvine, among others, to be southwestern English in dialect; see Irvine, *Old English Homilies.* Several of the homilies are based on earlier exemplars, so this may not add much more to the evidence. For a fuller assessment, see Conti, "Preaching Scripture and Apocrypha"; and Conti and Da Rold, "Bodley 343."

25 Ker, *Catalogue*, 473: "(xiii ?)."

Cathedral, where he is commemorated in an Ely book, the twelfth-century *Liber Eliensis*.

Another marginal addition to Bodley 343 provides more evidence for other possible localizations of the manuscript. There is, for example, a connection with St. Wulfhad, an obscure pre-conquest English saint, whose cult is most closely associated with Stone in Staffordshire.[26] At folio iiir of Bodley 343, someone called "Guilelmo Rotori" recorded a charge for his work ("per travayl ii s"), and left readers with this laudatory hymn praising Wulfhad as a new Isaac, a true martyr of God:

> Gaude stirpe regia insignita Mercia,
> In te dum egregia fiunt sacrificia,
> Pater sumit gladium, iam strues paratur,
> Wlphadus, pro Isaac agnus ymolatur,
> Wlferus, alter Abraham, ascendit in montem,
> Parcit prior filio, ferit hic insontem.
> Regnum spernis, in supernis regnans gloriose.
> Nos tuere martir vere Dei preciose.

> Rejoice, Mercia, adorned with your royal family,
> In you already were made extraordinary sacrifices.
> The father takes up the sword, the offering pile is prepared.
> Wulfhad, like Isaac, the sacrificial lamb,
> Wulfhere, another Abraham, ascends the mountain.
> He spares the firstborn son, he strikes the innocent one.
> You reject the earthly kingdom; now reigning in high honour.
> Protect us, true precious martyr of God.

This poem suggests further evidence for a West Midlands and perhaps specifically Staffordshire affiliation or connection for Bodley 343. Wulfhad was the murdered brother of St. Werburgh, patron now of Chester Cathedral, and associated with that city since the later Middle Ages. Both saints had something of a resurgence in the twelfth century (along with other pre-

26 St. Wulfhad was a saint associated with Stone, a daughter-house to Kenilworth. The Kenilworth Missal (discussed by Pfaff in *Music and Manuscripts*) contains Wulfhad, though written in the thirteenth century. Wulfhad is also celebrated in the Haughmond Gradual, now at Shrewsbury; and Cambridge, Corpus Christi College, MS 433, the Cluniac Chronicle, related to the Haughmond Gradual, seems to have originated at Much Wenlock in the thirteenth century. See Pfaff, *Liturgy*, 277. The earliest hand in this manuscript, Corpus 433, is dated by the Parker on the Web website, following James's *Catalogue*, to the early thirteenth century and clearly illustrates the closed top bow of **a** and **t** where the stem pierces the cross-stroke; see fol. 21, for example. It should be noted, though, that the writing grid is "below top line," and thus possibly dateable to before ca. 1230.

Figure 7. Decorated initial M, in Oxford, Bodleian Library, Bodley MS 343, fol. 158r. © The Bodleian Library, Oxford.

Conquest saints appropriated by Norman prelates). But as Alan Thacker has recently detailed, Werburgh's cult was most prominent at Ely Cathedral in the post-Conquest period.[27] Lives of Werburgh were written into a number of manuscripts written at Ely, including the *Liber Eliensis* manuscript—Cambridge, Trinity College, MS O. 2. 1; London, British Library, Cotton MS Caligula A. viii; and Cambridge, Corpus Christi College, MS 393, for example.

Further evidence moves Bodley 343 away from Worcester and towards another religious centre. Among the black, red, blue, or green decorated *litterae notabiliores* (the notable letters) in the manuscript are unusual capitals which are geometric or floriated. The capitals **D** and **M** (see figure 7 for the form of **M**) are an amalgam of designs with dots surrounded by circles or lines; hatched elaborate embellishments; and a "raised finger" decorative motif that is distinctive (Fig. 7). These may be linked with an earlier English manuscript that is assigned first to Christ Church, Canterbury, but then to Ely—Cambridge University Library, MS Ii. 1. 33 at fol. 58r. There are also *textual* analogies between this manuscript and eschatological texts in Bodley 343, which suggest this Ely connection is worth pursuing.[28] It ought not to be a surprise—despite the geographical distance—that these Benedictine monastic institutions would be connected both through English vernacular textual production and palaeographical elements.

The notable motif of the "raised finger" (my own label for this device), a decorative finial emerging from a floriated base, is present in the penwork of enlarged capitals in Bodley 343. In the hands of Bodley 343's artist, the motif is relatively inexpert, unlike in the hands of other decorators, such

27 Thacker, "St. Waerburh," 443–66n20.

28 Heningham, "Old English Precursors of 'The Worcester Fragments.'"

as that of London, British Library, Cotton MS Claudius E. i, a contemporary manuscript produced in Tewkesbury in the fourth quarter of the twelfth century and first of the thirteenth.[29] It is also found, with other similarities of *mise-en-page* to Bodley 343 in the Hereford manuscript, Hereford Cathedral Library, MS O. 7. 3, dated to the end of the twelfth century. This decorative finial is distinctive and a close parallel is also found in a manuscript from St. Frideswide's in Oxford—Paris, Bibliothèque nationale de France, MS français 24766, made in 1212–1214. The use of this motif together with other types of decorated initials in Bodley 343 and these referenced manuscripts is a reminder that whole teams produced books in this period and later; that monastic institutions from the second-half of the twelfth century increasingly hired scribes and artists to come and assist in the manufacture of books; and that variety and invention in modes of textual production appear to be of the moment in the last decades of the twelfth and first decades of the thirteenth centuries. It seems likely, then, that Oxford, Bodleian Library, Bodley MS 343 may not be from Worcester after all, despite containing English texts;[30] scholars could profitably look elsewhere—Tewkesbury, Cirencester, Ely, or lesser-known houses—for more evidence towards the localization of this important manuscript; and the weight of evidence based on this decorative device points towards Hereford, since it appears in manuscripts known to have been produced there.[31]

More work on scripts and decoration from ca. 1170–1250, and especially research that highlights the *varieties* of script in this period, will open up a whole range of scribal practices and locations of production. Matthew Aiello's recent extensive article on the forms of English vernacular script in the thirteenth century demonstrates that for writers of English in that century *variety* is a condition of the writing environments of the day.[32] These scribes, in spite of a general scholarly belief that the most *de luxe* volumes were written in the highest grade of Gothic *textura*, seemed often to just get on with the task at hand. What is interesting (and Aiello comments on this) is how

29 London, British Library, Cotton MS Claudius E. i is fully digitized on the British Library's digital manuscripts website.

30 There is a quite understandable tendency to think first of Worcester as the place of origin for English manuscripts from the (south)west of England in the post-Conquest period. See further the essays in Scase, *Essays in Manuscript Geography*, including my own "Bishops and their Texts," at 13–28.

31 See Mynors and Thomson, *Manuscripts of Hereford*, Plates 78(a) and (b) and 79 for other examples of devices found in manuscripts now at Hereford, some of which certainly originated there.

32 Aiello, "English Vernacular Script."

palaeography textbooks and monographs teach through typologies that fit particular kinds of textual production—the liturgical, the diplomatic—and such an approach, convenient though it may be, cannot fully account for the diversity of performances in between these genres and forms.

Aiello is focused on English, but actually these comments on the variety of scripts and hands in the thirteenth century are equally valid for Latin and French textual manufacture. Gothic *textualis*, or *textura*, or book hand, does not dominate book production: not even close. And it is not in *textura* that scholars find innovation and change in the development of script; that is found in the less formal hands, even those that share the same space of the folio with the finest *textura*. In London, British Library, Cotton MS Claudius B. ii, for example, a late twelfth-century manuscript from Cirencester that includes Alan of Tewkesbury's collection of the Letters of the recently martyred Thomas Becket, contemporary scribes writing in the margins of the book exemplify the more informal type of book hand with charter hand features alongside the Gothic *textura* of the main body of writing.[33] There is no doubt that distinctive scripts had distinctive functions throughout the medieval period, but there is far greater variety, flexibility and innovation than standard accounts of palaeography permit. The issue with medieval script is similar to that of periodization in the modern academy, or perceived linguistic hierarchies; that is, these categories can be helpful, but they are also limiting and unrepresentative of how the majority of medieval writers and artisans went about their work. Eric Weiskott in his most recent book, *Meter and Modernity in English Verse, 1350–1650*, questions the utility of periodization as a mode of analysis of change;[34] some years ago, in arguing for the vitality of English in the twelfth century and in the opening chapters of this book, I asked similar questions of the scholarly divides created by labels that emerge not just from periodization, but also categories like "Old" and "Middle" in English.[35] Ardis Butterfield has asked us to think about languages—English, Latin, French—as belonging on a spectrum of linguistic possibility at this time and not as persistently distinctive modes of expression.[36] We might usefully think about script in similarly connective and less hierarchized ways, because, while change does happen over time, it does not tidily map onto modern classifications of script, history, discipline, or language.

---

33 The manuscript is digitized on the British Library digital manuscripts website.

34 Weiskott, *Meter and Modernity*.

35 I have made this point many times since the late 1990s. See, for example, Treharne, "Reading from the Margins."

36 Butterfield, "The Dream of Language."

Arbiters of Choice

This spectrum of possibility and the recognition of flexibility of choice reflects a reality that would have been more recognizable, perhaps, to participants in writing communities in the High Middle Ages. But to whom does this set of possibilities apply; who are these participants in literary cultures, especially those involved in the physical act of writing? Who are the people accessing, using, transforming, creating, and inspiring book production with its associated and orbiting environments of textual production?

For the later medieval period, Sebastian Sobecki has been able to narrow down communities of vernacular writing practice in London after 1400 by focusing on the personnel—many of them named individuals—involved in the facture of literary and documentary texts.[37] There is some evidence for those who wrote, and when and where they wrote, in the *earlier* medieval period, but in much less density and with far fewer named scribes. Of the names of writers that modern scholars know, a great deal can be learned about textual production in specifically monastic and ecclesiastical circles. Where there is a name but not a location for a scribe, we should bear in mind that writing could occur outside the religious institution as well as within it. At the same time, though, to have a charter issued by a central figure—even one as significant as the Magna Carta sealed by King John—does not mean it had to be written by chancery or non-monastically affiliated scribes, as will be discussed below. It is more useful perhaps, for the later twelfth and earlier thirteenth centuries, to think of variety and nimbleness in scribal production broadly conceived; some of what survives illustrates a pragmatic response to need in terms of writing practices. Recognizing medieval writing outside the categories of script analysed in standard palaeography handbooks allows scholars to think in different ways about writing communities.[38] Would removing some of the focus on "scriptoria" (or even "workshops") permit one to think more broadly in terms—instead of central figures—of book-owners and keepers, not *in place* of institutional ownership, but *as well as*. Indeed, what does it mean to *own* a book in this pre-1250 period?

---

37 Sobecki, "Communities of Practice."

38 Standard English handbooks and introductions to medieval writing, all of which are tremendously valuable in the classroom for beginners, include Brown, *A Guide to Western Historical Scripts*; Ullman, *Ancient Writing and Its Influence*; and Clemens and Graham, *An Introduction to Manuscript Studies*. See also Treharne, "Manuscript Sources of Old English Poetry."

In his "Handwriting in English Books" in the *Cambridge History of the Book*, Malcolm Parkes reminded readers of the reality of book production in the twelfth century:

> Organized copying by members of a community usually lasted only for short periods: once a community had built up its collection of texts, organized copying was abandoned, and with it some of the distinctive features in local handwriting.[39]

Parkes is undoubtedly right when it comes to, say, the eleventh century. Some years ago, in relation to Leofric, bishop of Exeter, and his circle of scribes, I followed up on a comment of T. A. M. Bishop's that Leofric had his own Episcopal Library.[40] He created this library, or had it created, when he moved his bishopric from Crediton to Exeter in 1050. Countering comments by earlier scholars that Leofric had the canons of Exeter write the books he required, I postulated that Leofric's writing office was temporary—exigent and concerted—established only to produce what the bishop needed to go about his work.[41] Eight scribes seem principally to be working on manuscripts for Leofric simultaneously, writing with a developed house-style and in a relatively short period of time. These books made by this cohort of professionals are among those gathered by Leofric, some of which were donated to Exeter Cathedral Chapter on his death in 1072, as is well known.

I argued that it is unlikely to be Exeter canons who predominated in this writing office; rather, they may have been colleagues that Leofric, as former

39 Parkes, "Handwriting in English Books," 111. Parkes also commented: "[In the twelfth century] Some communities hired scribes (laymen or secular clergy) to supplement the efforts of the monks, as at St. Albans, and, later, at Abingdon where hired scribes produced copies of patristic texts whilst the monks copied books for the *opus Dei*. Monks also compiled and maintained the records required for running a monastery and protecting its privileges."

40 Bishop uses this term "Episcopal Library" in his "Notes on Cambridge Manuscripts: Part II." At 199 he discusses the Episcopal Library at Exeter, which survived for several centuries following Leofric's death. The precise meaning of "Episcopal Library" is not made clear. I would suggest this means a library separate from that to which the canons had access. See further, Treharne, "Producing a Library."

41 Treharne, "Producing a Library." See also the important work of Drage, "Bishop Leofric and the Exeter Cathedral Chapter." She identifies some sixteen scribes at work in this period, with the assumption that the scribes were also canons. This number of scribes suggests a well-staffed scriptorium, though whether these scribes were also canons is debatable. Barlow, *English Episcopal Acta XI*, lv, suggests that the number of canons Leofric established in 1050 might have been as small as five. See also Edwards, *The Secular Cathedrals*, 260.

chancellor for Edward the Confessor, drafted in from the proto-chancery. Perhaps there is something similar happening at this time in other episcopal residences throughout eleventh-century England, an arrangement extending, one might imagine, into the twelfth century, sometimes in concert with dedicated and deliberate scribal effort on behalf of an institution that may have ebbed and flowed with demand. Perhaps, too, that demand can be seen to coincide with new prelates coming into their offices, setting up their own circle of scribes for immediate textual production?

This transient and nimble cohort of learned professionals is certainly what can be understood by the entourage of Thomas Becket one hundred years later than Leofric. Not only had Becket been chancellor for Henry II, gathering expertise and professional clerical personnel around him, some of whom were themselves translated into positions of pre-eminence in the English Church, but also, he had a high level of scribal proficiency himself. In his years in exile in 1164–1166, Becket's biographers, and especially those at Pontigny, reveal he surrounded himself with learned men, who formed a bookish circle of companions, as Laura Cleaver and Anne Duggan have both elucidated so well in the collection devoted to *Herbert of Bosham*.[42] The archbishop himself copied books, received manuscripts and texts produced at his request, and, as Herbert of Bosham reported, Becket used his time to focus intently intellectually and spiritually on the Epistles and Psalms.[43] The writing activities among this group were evidently pressured and intensive, given the numbers of letters that were created in addition to the books. While being in exile was presumably akin to the scholarly focus provided by an academic's sabbatical, a detailed picture emerges in the writings of Becket's biographers and entourage of the varied business of the writing community.

Some of the fruits of this community's work are made evident in the account of Becket's murder in 1170. William FitzStephen, a contemporary biographer of Becket's who was present at the time provides details of the assailants' acts of vandalism and theft:

> [the assailants] broke open his chests and book-cases; they seized gold and silver vessels, money, gold signet rings, papal bulls, books, precious materials…They entered the room of the clerics and carried off their garments, books, money, baggage, together with all their household furnishings.[44]

---

42 Duggan, "Master Herbert" and Cleaver, "Pages Covered with as Many Tears as Notes."

43 Cleaver, "Pages Covered with as Many Tears as Notes," 66.

44 William FitzStephen, *Life of Becket*. See also https://blogs.bl.uk/digitisedmanuscripts/2017/09/wheres-walter.html on a contemporary scribe, Walter Mileto, and his writing.

That books are part of the personal belongings of an archbishop and his clerics will come as no surprise, but the ubiquity of the book in these circles says more again about writing and book-owning practices in this period. Perhaps one of the most famous instances of a book-producing bishop, along with Wulfstan I and Leofric from pre-Conquest England, is St. Anselm himself. In Chapter 19 of his *Life of St. Anselm: Archbishop of Canterbury*, Anselm's biographer Eadmer deals with "the books Anselm wrote, and what first happened to the one which called the *Proslogion*."[45] In this account, Eadmer reveals Anselm's intellectual and spiritual struggles with the genesis of the account of God's existence in the *Proslogion*. We are told that:

> Then suddenly one night during matins the grace of God illuminated his heart, the whole matter became clear to his mind, and a great joy and exultation filled his inmost being. Thinking therefore that other also would be glad to know what he had found, he immediately and ungrudgingly wrote it on writing tablets and gave them to one of the brethren of the monastery for safe-keeping. After a few days he asked the monk who had charge of them for the tablets. The place where they had been laid was searched, but they were not found. The brethren were asked in case anyone had taken them, but in vain. And to this day no one has been found who has confessed that he knew anything about them. Anselm wrote another draft on the same subject on other tablets, and handed them over to the same monk for more careful keeping. He placed them once more by his bed, in a more secret place, and the next day—having no suspicion of any mischance—he found them scattered on the floor beside his bed and the wax which was on them strewn about in small pieces. After the tablets had been picked up and the wax collected together, they were taken to Anselm. He pieced together the wax and recovered the writing, though with difficulty. Fearing now that be some carelessness it might be altogether lost, he ordered it, in the name of the Lord, to be copied onto parchment.

The operation of writing practices here is revealing. First, a senior prelate is inspired to write a book himself and does so as that inspiration strikes, using writing materials that are close by. In this case, the impermanent and fragile drafting tools and substrate prove easily lost not once, but twice. When the writing is to be made expeditiously but permanently, the task is assigned to a scribe. Yet we know that Anselm did more than write drafts himself; earlier, in Chapter 15, Eadmer narrates that when a monk was possessed by a demon, a fellow "went in haste to Anselm, who was busy in the cloister correcting books:" "Riculfus...ad Anselmum qui tunc in claustro emendandis libris" (Riculf went to Anselm who was then in the cloister emending books).[46]

45 Southern, *The Life of St. Anselm*, 28–31.

46 Southern, *The Life of St. Anselm*, 24.

Numerous other prelates and learned scholars are known to have corrected books, too—whether their own or other writers'. The handwriting of some senior ecclesiastics is present in manuscripts, and accounts written about some bishops and abbots confirm that they engaged in correction. Pre-Conquest correctors included Ælfric, Abbot of Eynsham, the prolific Old English homilist and monk (d. 1010); Wulfstan, bishop of Worcester and archbishop of York, statesman, law-maker, and sermon-writer (d. 1023); Leofric, bishop of Exeter (d. 1072)—to whom I've already referred; and Coleman, the later eleventh-century Worcester monk and St. Wulfstan's chancellor. Then, of the many prelates, one can note the thirteenth-century St. Edmund of Abingdon, of whom we are told: "The blessed Edmund used to detest idleness and sloth, and was himself always occupied either in praying or meditating, or in the correcting of books, or in hearing confessions, or in solving questions put to him by this brethren, or in deciding suits which had arisen, lest the enemy of mankind should ever find him unbusied with good works and idle."[47]

Most manuscripts show signs of having been corrected. Sometimes this work is done by the scribe and/or author themselves. In the case of Herbert of Bosham, Laura Cleaver and Stella Panayotova note that Herbert corrected and annotated the volumes of his own work on Peter Lombard's *Glossa magnatura* in, perhaps, the 1170s. In Cambridge, Corpus Christi College, MS 303, ca. 1150 from Rochester, the manuscript's corrector is also the rubricator and third scribe. In his *Catalogue of Manuscripts containing Anglo-Saxon*, Neil Ker calls this supervisor "the less good hand." But it is this "less good hand" (by which Ker might mean the hand is more irregular and idiosyncratic than the set late Caroline Minuscule illustrated by the manuscript's other two scribes) that oversees the book's compilation and composition and who illustrates in his stints the most up-to-date and independent writing. I dealt with the problem of value judgements like "less good" in the field of palaeography in "The Good, the Bad, and the Ugly" some years ago, but they continue to affect how we interpret and evaluate scribal performance in the overall system of writing practices.[48]

In terms of manuscripts, one might argue that the inclination to define scribal performance by calligraphic and aesthetic values *without explicitly stating these criteria* has detrimentally affected how scholars regard not just hands of individual actors, but all those who are neither clearly diplomatically engaged in the copying of administratively-originating documentation

---

47 Ward, *The Life of St. Edmund*, 96.

48 Treharne, "'The Good, the Bad, the Ugly'"; and Treharne, "'Terrible Letters.'"

nor attempting to emulate formal book hand—either Caroline Minuscule or Gothic. Other scribal performances, and necessarily all non-Latin scribal performance, are thus judged by *lack*, by *absence* of the attributes of formality and high grade in relation to experienced scribes of book hand.

This deficit is in error, really. Some of the least visually appealing handwriting belongs to the most brilliant scholars—to a Wulfstan of York, or a St. Hugh of Lincoln, for example,[49] or to the Tremulous Hand of Worcester and the other slightly shaky exponents of contemporary poetic and musical art, as in Oxford, Bodleian Library, MS Bodley 343. Book hand can be calligraphically expert and aesthetically pleasing, and untidy set hands can belong to outstanding intellectuals, but it is most often in the work of the correctors, the annotators, the glossators, the commentators, and the folio-fillers that innovation and fresh movement in handwriting both begins and rubs along happily with the more obviously enviable expert exponents of *textura*. As usual, all the exciting stuff is happening in the margins.

Herbert of Bosham's manuscripts from the third quarter of the twelfth century like Cambridge, Trinity College, MS B. 5. 4, partly annotated and corrected in Bosham's hand, fols. 50v–51r, allow us to see how his commentary and the layers of notes provide diagnostic information for scripts that are yet to emerge in a widespread fashion (Fig. 8). Such an observation is important not simply for the reassessment of the means by which scholars audit and assess manuscript production, but also because it insists that scholars think again about writing practices, the skills required to write by those who might be senior prelates and intellectuals or those who might only write when they had to.[50] Many scribes, whether a senior prelate, a nun, or a rural priest, are described as "poor" or "untrained" when if they had the capacity to write at all they simply could *not have been* either "poor" scribes or "untrained" practitioners. Orietta Da Rold's fundamental questions in her "Working with Paper" asks what constitutes scribal training and what is meant by "professional scribes." These are essential queries for beginning to unpick the hierarchizing effect of established categories of book production that begin with *textura* as the most important script and move down through a list of aesthetically impelled classifications.[51]

---

49 The latter is contained in Lincoln Cathedral Chapter Library, MS 107, fol. 3r. See Thomson, *Catalogue of the Manuscripts of Lincoln*.

50 For which see Afterwords below.

51 Da Rold, *Paper in Medieval England*, especially Chapter 8.

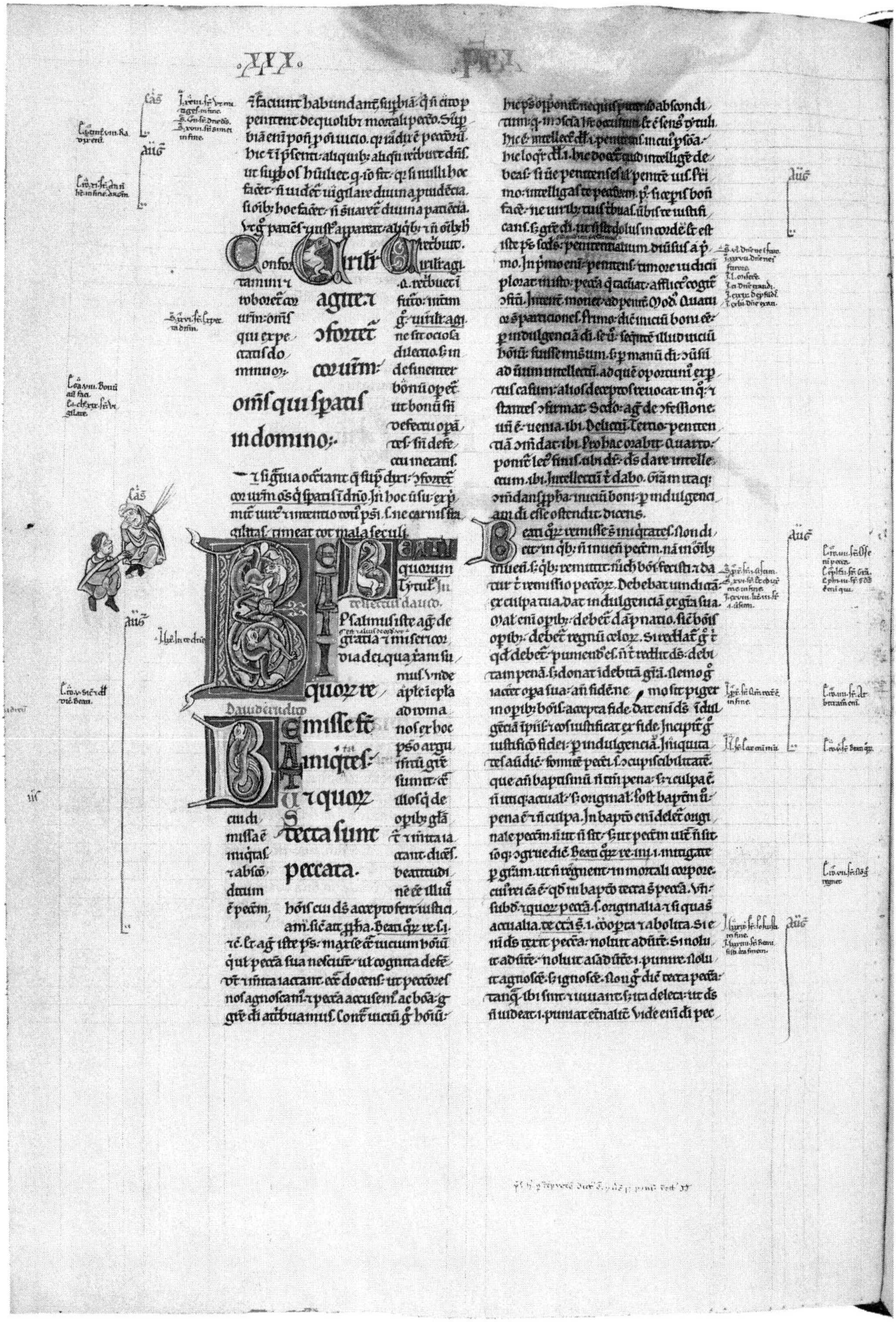

Figure 8. Cambridge, Trinity College, MS B. 5. 4, fol. 84v. © Reproduced by permission of the Masters and Fellows, Trinity College, Cambridge.

Textual Positioning

Varieties of script form the basis for some suppositions about the types of places from which manuscripts and documents originate, as well as for the topologizing of those textual objects themselves. In 2015, Andrew Prescott and I revealed through a close study of the four surviving engrossments of the Magna Carta that the Salisbury Magna Carta was likely to have been produced at Salisbury Cathedral, rather than within a centralized administrative context.[52] We argue that the Salisbury Magna Carta was written by a Salisbury scribe working in and for Old Sarum (and from 1220, Salisbury) Cathedral, a secular cathedral with canons, a dean, and a bishop. By analysing the hands in other certain contemporary Salisbury manuscripts and documents, particularly *The Register of St. Osmund* (ca. 1220), I suggest that similarities between hands in that book and the hand of the Salisbury Magna Carta show such distinctive shared characteristics as to intimate the Salisbury origin of the Magna Carta. This necessarily calls into question scholarly understanding how major administrative texts were disseminated in the later Middle Ages.[53]

Of the four 1215 engrossments of Magna Carta, the one whose appearance differs most obviously from the others is that in the Salisbury Cathedral archives (which has the siglum *S*), since it is the only one not in a documentary hand[54] (Fig. 9). Sir James Holt commented of it: "The other three are plainly in a Chancery hand; S not so—not, at least, until the scribe of S is discovered at work in other chancery documents. His hand is too 'bookish.'"[55]

---

52 Treharne and Prescott, "The Origin and Context of the Salisbury Magna Carta," at http://historyoftexttechnologies.blogspot.com/2015_06_01_archive.html and http://digitalriffs.blogspot.com/2015/06/the-origin-and-context-of-salisbury_13.html.

53 In this article, I focused on the palaeography and Andrew Prescott closely examined the history, form of the engrossments, and the particular features of each of the four extant witnesses of the 1215 charter: the four engrossments are London, British Library, Cotton MS Augustus ii.106; British Library, Cotton Charter xiii.31a; the Salisbury Cathedral Library and Chapter, Magna Carta; and the Lincoln Magna Carta.

54 See the major collaborative scholarly project from 2015, spearheaded by Carpenter and Vincent, *The Magna Carta Project* at https://magnacartaresearch.org/.

55 Holt, *Magna Carta*, 374. We have to assume that "too bookish" means the *textura* elements of the script render it not cursive enough to be considered a product of the chancery.

Figure 9. Salisbury Magna Carta. Salisbury Cathedral Dean and Chapter. Reproduced by permission of Salisbury Cathedral Dean and Chapter. Photograph © Russell Sach.

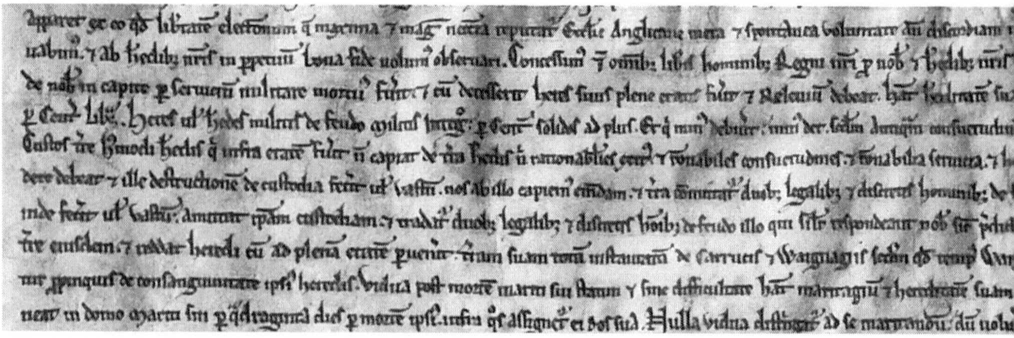

Figure 10. Detail, Salisbury Magna Carta, Salisbury Cathedral Dean and Chapter. Reproduced by permission of Salisbury Cathedral Dean and Chapter. Photograph © Russell Sach.

Collins is even more trenchant: "Just as the text of S is inferior to that of the other exemplars, so its script is the least convincing. To my eye it rather suggests a date a decade or so later than 1215 and smacks of an ecclesiastical scriptorium. It seems to me to be similar in type (but earlier than) the hand of the charter of the Dean and Chapter of Salisbury of 1244 in the British Museum, Add. Ch. 7500."[56] However, Collins noted that Charles Johnson and Hilary Jenkinson, two leading authorities on documentary script, would not rule out the possibility that *S* was written in the royal chancery in 1215, and Collins emphasized the variability of scripts in later reissues of Magna Carta. In 1981, Daphne Stroud challenged the authenticity of *S*, writing that "Both in text and script S is the odd man out of the four manuscripts. It is written in the careful and dignified script employed at this period for copying books, not in the business hand normally used for chancery documents in which (the other 1215 charters) are written. It also has more textual variations than the other three."[57] She suggested it was a copy made and taken to Salisbury by a future canon there. These scholars' ruling out of locations of production based purely on formality of script is problematic.

Emily Naish, the archivist at Salisbury Cathedral, made the important discovery in 2015 that there is a copy of the text of *S* on fols. 5v–7v of the Salisbury Cathedral Cartulary, "Liber Evidentiarum C," compiled before 1284.[58] This shows that *S* has been at Salisbury since the thirteenth century. While until 2015 there had been discussion of the dating of *S*, there

56 Collins, "The Documents of the Great Charter of 1215," 270n3.

57 Stroud, "Salisbury's Magna Carta," 51.

58 Carpenter, "The Cartulary Copies at Lincoln and Salisbury": http://magnacarta.cmp.uea.ac.uk/read/feature_of_the_month/May_2015_2.

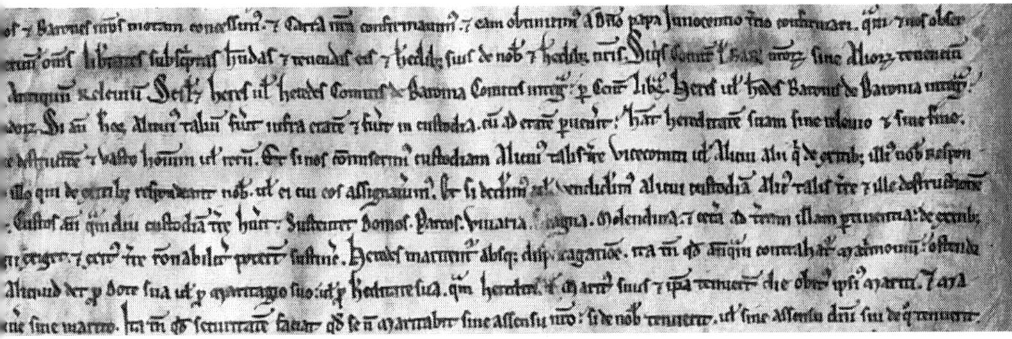

had been no sustained attempt to localize the hand. My further examination of known Salisbury hands in the first decades of the thirteenth century, though, strongly indicates that *S* was written by a scribe from Salisbury Cathedral (or, rather, its pre-1220 institutional precursor at Old Sarum), rather than a chancery or centralized scribe. The Salisbury Magna Carta hand is both entirely commensurate with other hands datable to ca. 1215 and exemplifies that book hand could be used alongside charter hand within a single institutional context and that, in fact, the distinction in intention and function between the hands was not always clear-cut.[59] This has important implications for the broader discussion of what kinds of scripts were used, where, when, and by whom. Scribes had choices about which scripts they used that did not always tally with the distinctions highlighted in present-day palaeography handbooks: charter hands for charters; book hands for books. Both the Salisbury Magna Carta and other textual objects from this period demonstrate that above all else scribal output could vary significantly and depart from expectations one would have gained from reading scholars' script taxonomies.

The hand of *S* can be compared, in the first instance, with other contemporary documents, including London, British Library, Additional MS 4838, *The Articles of the Barons*, issued in 1215 (as well as with the three other 1215 Magna Carta engrossments, of course).[60] Additional MS 4838 is written in a legible, cursive charter hand, with its slightly backward-looking aspect; and a duct illustrating typical thicker ascenders and curvilinear strokes. Many ascenders are looped and descenders of **p** and **q** are tapered, curving slightly to the left. By contrast to this charter hand, and as noted by

59 This is further borne out by research into earlier thirteenth-century Mortuary Rolls by Treharne and Fafinski in *Medieval Networks of Memory*: https://medievalnetworks.github.io/mnm/.

60 Additional MS. 4838 is digitally available at the British Library digital manuscripts website.

all scholars who have worked on the four 1215 Magna Carta versions, Salisbury's charter is written in a mostly Gothic *textura* or book hand rather than a diplomatic hand and this is important for comparative examination purposes.[61] The evidence is more formality and less currency or cursivity than one might expect from a documentary text; its formality is demonstrated in its upright aspect, numerous pen lifts between letters, and general restraint. Ascenders are usually tagged or slightly wedged to the left; descenders are short and finish with a small tick to the right (Fig. 10).

Significant scribal characteristics include the persistent use of double-compartment **a**, sometimes with an enlarged bow in final position ("Carta," line 5; "custodia") or initial position (line 9 "aliquid," line 14); **d** is round-backed with a curve to the right at the end of the ascender, or straight-backed with a finish of equal floriation; the tongue of **e** is very slightly elongated in final position. The letter **g** takes a variety of forms and is one of the most important characteristics of this hand: it is either relatively small with an equal sized closed tail and bowl ("maritagium," line 14—a typical book hand type); or, also as in book hand, it has a closed tail which is angular on the left (line 13, "exiget"); or, and most frequently and notably, the tail finishes with a flourish, which loops under the tail-end and sweeps up to the bowl (line 4, "Burgo"; line 7, "Regni"). Interestingly, a small majuscule **r** occurs most often in front of variant forms of "Rex," but also in "Relevium" (line 8). A slightly later manuscript, Cambridge, Corpus Christi College, 275, a composite manuscript that has a thirteenth-century *Life of Thomas Becket* inserted between later texts (it is ca. 1230, given that it is written below top line), also shows this feature, such as at fol. 233aR/11 and 12, "Regis" (and elsewhere, including in medial position where it is ligatured with a ("baʀonia," fol. 233bV, line 25). Of this form, Derolez comments: "The majuscule r (R) occasionally present in Praegothica is found much more rarely in Textualis, except in a few early English manuscripts."[62] He gives an unillustrated example in his footnote 80 of a manuscript, dated pre-1201. It is likely, given the evidence presented here, that this feature is found rather later than Derolez suspects.

Ligatures include the 2-shaped **r** in **or** combination; a characteristic form of the crossed 2-shaped *r*, indicating *–orum* (line 5, "aliorum"); and **ct** where the ligature is formed from by a curved stroke extending from the

---

61 It is available in a rather odd yellowy digital aspect: <http://www.bl.uk/britishlibrary/~/media/bl/global/pressrelease/2015/february/magna-carta-1215–salisbury-cathedral.jpg>.

62 Derolez, *The Palaeography of Gothic*, 91.

top of **c**'s bow to the top of **t**. Biting letters include the common **d+e**, **b+b**, **d+d**, and **p+p**. Other noteworthy characteristics include the usually crossed Tironian *nota*, which sits on the line, together with the occasional uncrossed version (lines 5 and 6 "7 heredibus" and "7 Barones" demonstrate each respectively); barred capitals; the open-topped form of suprascript **a** predominantly used to denote abbreviations like *qua-* or *–ra* ("quam," line 6; "libras," line 8. This seems to be a consistently earlier practice than the flat-topped version of the mark.); the dashed double **i**; and a consistently curved abbreviation stroke.

There is far more one could say, but this collection of data, taken *in toto*, is sufficient to build a strong case for the production of *S*, the Salisbury Magna Carta, by a Salisbury scribe. Several comparanda support this claim, among them the existence of multiple Salisbury scribes writing in manuscripts and diplomata that are, and always have been, *in situ* in the archive that created them. Such a finding emerges from a comparison of palaeographical characteristics between *S* and certain scribes of *The Register of St. Osmund*, now housed in Salisbury Cathedral Archive (Fig. 11).[63] This *Register*, until recently deposited in the Wiltshire County Record Office, is generally dated to ca. 1220, presumably because that is the date of the foundation of the new cathedral building at Salisbury. It may, of course, have been begun slightly earlier in readiness for the move from Old Sarum to the present site, since the volume contains the fullest extant text of Bishop (and St.) Osmund's *Consuetudinary*, including descriptions of the roles of the cathedral's major officers and liturgical rites. It seems likely that the *Register* was compiled and maintained as both guide to the organizational practices of the cathedral and as a repository of the privileges, liberties, and possessions of the institution. Following the *Consuetudinary*, the volume becomes, effectively, a cartulary with many documents added as the thirteenth century progressed. Taking stock in this way during the years of planning and implementing the move—a move initiated by Richard Poore, bishop of Salisbury 1217 to 1228, and granted in 1219 by papal indulgence—made absolute sense to ensure a secure record intended for the cathedral's reference and archive.

The earliest scribe in the *Register* copied the opening folios containing the Statutes and Regulations of the cathedral. His is a book hand of greater formality than that associated with Salisbury's Magna Carta. Consistent with other *textura* of the period, the aspect is generally upright, though sometimes rather backward-tilting; the ascenders and descenders generally

63 See http://www.sarumcustomary.org.uk/exploring/PDF_files/1%20OCO/OCO-L.pdf.

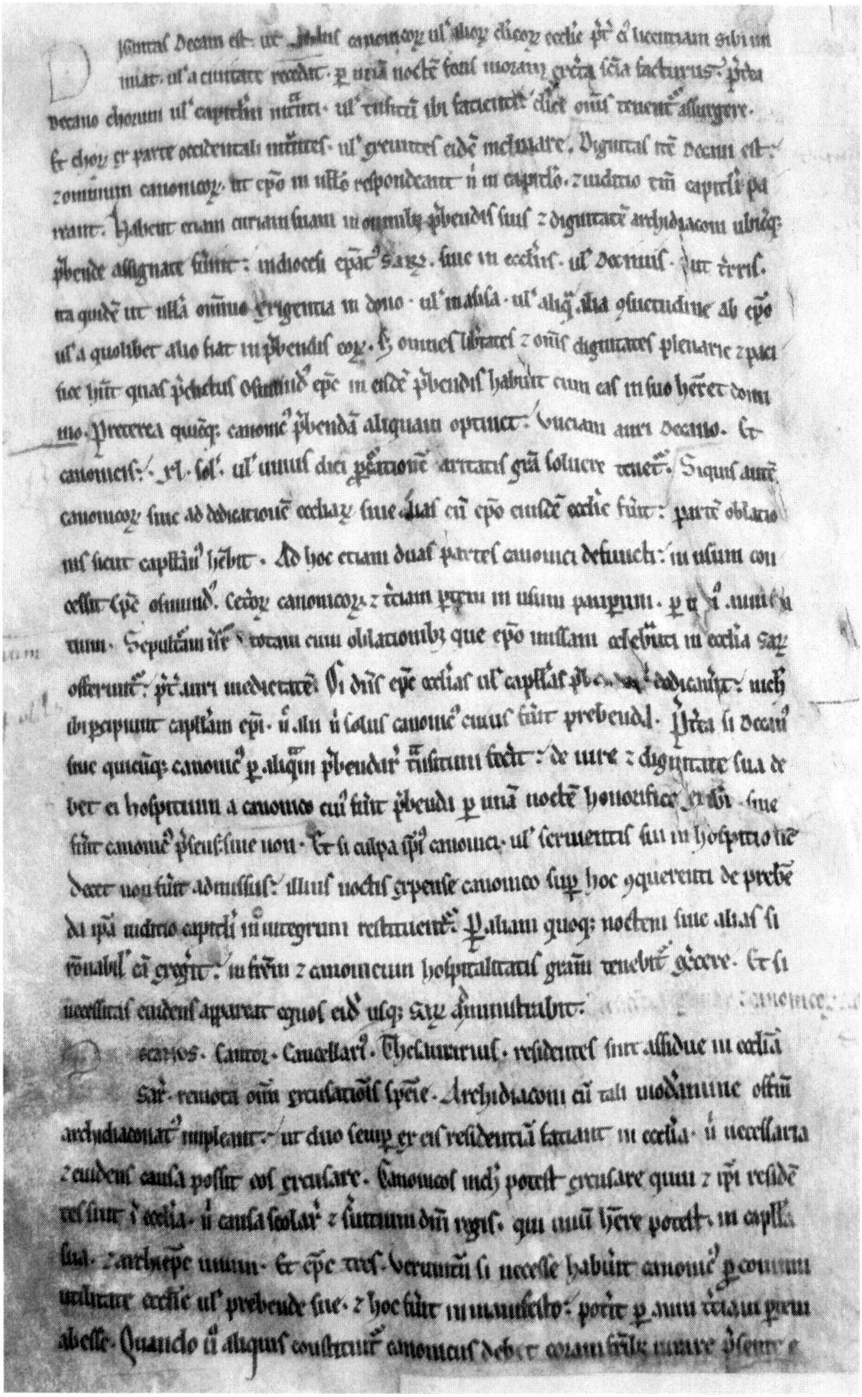

Figure 11. *Register of St. Osmund*, Salisbury Cathedral Dean and Chapter. Reproduced by permission of Salisbury Cathedral Dean and Chapter.

compact (and often lacking the flourish seen in *S*); the pen-angle about 30°. Two-compartment **a** predominates, and the occasional enlarged **a** makes a few appearances; straight-backed and round-backed **d** are used; the small 8-shaped **g** is most common. Like *S*, and many other examples, the left limb of **x** swoops under the preceding letter. There are frequent, but not ubiquitous barred majuscule forms. These increase in number as the manuscript's earliest scribe works through his multiple stints. His biting letters include **d+e** and double **p**. As in *S*, there is the occasional use of a conjoined enlarged **a** and **d** in "ad," where the ascender of round-backed **d** pierces the bow of **a**. In the early pages of the *Register*, the Tironian *nota* is not crossed; later hands illustrate varied usage that is sometimes crossed, and sometimes simply **7**. The suprascript **a** with a flat, closed top is most common in the introductory pages, but there are also instances of the open **a** seen in *S*. The macron, like *S*'s, is curved. Confirming a date of the first third of the century (and somewhat earlier, indeed) is the "above top line" format of the folio. While the hand is more laterally compressed than that of *S*, there are distinctive similarities, as one might expect.

The most notable preponderance of similarities between a scribe of the *Register* and Salisbury's Magna Carta comes quite far into the *Register* in a sequence of texts copied sometime after 1222. At pages 111–113, in a section on canonical behaviour, the scribe, whose hand is more cursive than that of *S*, nevertheless evinces similar forms of enlarged **a**, trailing **s**, majuscules, punctuation, and various other features. Of most significance, this scribe writes the very notable **g** with a tail that loops back upon itself to touch the bowl. This **g** is distinctive and allies the scribal practice of the Magna Carta hand with that of the *Register*'s scribe at these pages. It is seen elsewhere, but always in manuscripts or diplomata that are possibly slightly later than Magna Carta, including, obviously, the *Register* itself. It occurs in other diplomata associated with Salisbury, including a document issued to Salisbury by Archbishop Langton in ca. 1220 or a little earlier. Other instances of this particular form of **g** include Duchy of Lancaster, *Cartae Miscellaneae* 36, dated to 1229–1230;[64] London, British Library, Royal MS 14. C. vii, fol. 150, dated 1250–1259;[65] and in the closing lines of Cambridge, Corpus Christi College, MS 275, fols. 233a-n, which is post-1230, where the **g** is part of a final flourish at the foot of the writing grid. Its use in the Magna Carta is, then, among the earliest instances I have found.

64 See Hector, *Handwriting of English Documents*, Plate Va.

65 See Denholm-Young, *Handwriting in England and Wales*, Plate 12.

What emerges from this preliminary examination of Salisbury's *Register* and some of the cathedral chapter's documents is how very varied scribal hands are in this period, as Jenkinson and others have pointed out.[66] This is particularly so when the scripts are not the so-called highest grade of Gothic *textura* (*precissa, quadrata, semi-quadrata, rotunda*). Not only is it quite difficult to categorize the preponderance of hands beyond the broadest categories, but there are dramatic changes in appearance and letter-formation within approximately contemporary stints in similar contexts of production. This reflects "the proliferation of documents," as Clanchy says; the concomitant increase in numbers and levels of training of scribes; and the varieties of script commonly used for different kinds of writing, many manifested differently according to scribal proficiency and time.[67] But then the consistent and significant number of similar forms between the Salisbury Magna Carta and other known contemporary Salisbury scribes becomes a diagnostic of a shared writing environment. It is surely to this archival community that scholars should look to identify the common context for the Magna Carta's production, if not the very scribe himself.

It is indeed salutary, as Nicholas Vincent comments, to acknowledge that a solid, if not preponderant, proportion of diplomata produced were written by scribes attached to the beneficiary rather than to the king.[68] Supporting this, the palaeographical features consistently shared by some of the scribes of the *Register* and the scribe of *S* indicate that *S* was written by a scribe from the cathedral which has subsequently retained that instantiation of the Great Charter to this day. It is likely that recipients were able to present their own copies of Magna Carta for sealing by the chancery, opening up the questions of how Magna Carta and other governmental documents were disseminated in the Middle Ages. As this chapter has shown, there are new and broader questions to be asked about who participated in communities of writing within and without established ecclesiastical institutions; and how texts were produced, disseminated, and preserved. For scholars, the inherited frameworks of investigation—the script categories, the known places of manuscript production (like Worcester, in the case of post-Conquest English texts, for example)—are useful starting points, but there is more to be discovered by new investigations that take us beyond established categories and aesthetics of script, and rather poorly understood specifics, such as "scriptorium," "writing office," and "trained scribe."

---

66 See Jenkinson, *Palaeography and the Practical Study*.

67 Clanchy, *From Memory to Written Record*, 127–34.

68 Vincent, "Why 1199?," 31.

Reexamining scribal practices is important, especially now, as so much handwritten material appears online in digital form, available for scrutiny by scholars from their desks. It is essential that these manuscripts are treated as offering fresh opportunities for expanding what we know, rather than fitting into preexisting models. Reappraisal is needed for the work of scribes who *added* to manuscripts completed earlier thereby changing the functionality of the book in important ways. It might also be helpful to reappraise modern-day categories that group the writing of scribes in terms of formality, aesthetic, and even "grade." Many scribes—those writing day-to-day, and non-*de luxe*, books and documents—simply did not write according to modern palaeographers' retrospectively applied aesthetically impelled categories. Because of this, rather like writers who do not adhere to "standard" forms of language (as explained in earlier chapters), these scribes are derogated or considered "less good" than those writing formal *textura* or book hands. As this chapter has shown, once researchers move beyond the boundaries of received scholarly categories and classifications, information emerges that helps to effect exciting re-evaluations of what we think we know. Thus, variety and scribal *effort*—despite those scribes not having the best training, or sustained training, or spending their careers in regional writing environments—are worth close investigation; texts that appear not to be central to the perceived use of a manuscript are often essential clues to how books were understood and engaged with; and looking again at apparent evidence for dating, now that more manuscripts and documents are available for scrutiny than were ever accessible to our scholarly predecessors, can make a useful new contribution to accepted textual histories.

AFTERWORDS

INHERITED SCHOLARLY CATEGORIES are problematic as my case studies have shown. So much that is interesting for literary, historical, sociocultural, and material research falls into the gaps created by delimited areas of study: periodization used to create comfortable chunks for study; linguistic terminology used to create a narrative of language development that is neither borne out by the surviving evidence nor indicates how language was understood by manuscript compilers and scribes; generic distinction—legal, homiletic—used to create consonance and contiguities that might not be the most significant aspects of the texts; and categories of script, scribal competence, and points of manuscript origin that foster a too-tidy narrative of production and reception. This tidy narrative will be challenged as more original sources are digitized and deeper questions asked about textual communities in the later eleventh to earlier thirteenth centuries (as here), as well as at other points in the long history of western manuscript traditions and especially as they relate to a more inclusive, global story of the human record.

What will replace tidy narratives? As new textual materials are digitized online, new tools made available for transcription, translation, and analysis at scale, there is a pressing need for trained interpreters (scholars!) of these works and their physical contexts. New questions will emerge from fresh research that seeks to think outside delineated limits—whether generic, classificatory, periodized—and these new questions in turn will enhance scholars' knowledge of their primary sources and how they can be read. A world where manuscripts, documents, edited texts and translations are permitted to be evaluated on their own merits, or within systems of knowledge that are flexible and broad, is not out of reach or impossible. One final example can prove this point.

The Final Grade

I want to explore one short example challenging the unqualified use of hierarchies of calligraphic grade for scribal work in the premodern period to show how regarding an extant textual artefact in and for itself yields exciting results.[1] Privileging only the higher grades of script or more *de luxe* volumes diminishes the status of the *everyday* work of scribes, as I have hinted. So much manuscript material remains from the Middle Ages that reveals the day-to-day efforts of those scribes who did not attain the highest expertise and demonstrates unequivocally that different grades and models of script can coexist in multiple forms of writing. In Cambridge, St. John's College, MS N. 31, a Mortuary Roll dated to ca. 1215–1225, hundreds of scribal stints—all written on the same membranes of the same textual object—manifest intriguing variation. These entries made on behalf of ecclesiastical institutions show visible contiguities of what most palaeographers might typically label "poor" and "untidy" alongside "beautiful" and "neat," but their coexistence demands that different questions be asked of scribal effort in this period, so that more imaginative modes of investigation might emerge as a consequence (Fig. 12).

Medieval Networks of Memory, a Stanford Text Technologies project in collaboration with Professor Mateusz Fafinski, explores two earlier thirteenth-century English Mortuary Rolls: London, British Library, Egerton MS 2849 and Cambridge, St. John's College, MS N. 31.[2] These rolls contain entries written by representatives of male and female religious houses that contributed to messages of condolence and prayer on the death of senior religious colleagues—Lucy de Vere, Prioress of Hedingham, Essex, in the Egerton Roll, and Amphelisa, Prioress of Lillechurch, Kent, in MS N. 31. Building on Jean Dufour's foundational editorial work, this project has examined the hands visible in this and other rolls—an impressively diverse set of scribal efforts, despite the fact the two rolls were probably compiled within a relatively short space of time between ca. 1215–1229.[3] We have learned an immense amount from detailed digital analyses of individual features of the 450+ hands in both rolls, and about regional and institutional variation in scribal practice. Figure 12 of the Amphelisa Roll (MS N. 31) illustrates a sequence of monasteries and nunneries in Lincolnshire, a county where the most

1 See, for example, Gameson, "The Emergence of Formal Gothic Script in England."

2 The Egerton Roll is digitized by the British Library. See our preliminary work and findings at *Medieval Networks of Memory* and in the forthcoming article on these materials.

3 Dufour, *Recueil des Rouleaux des Morts*.

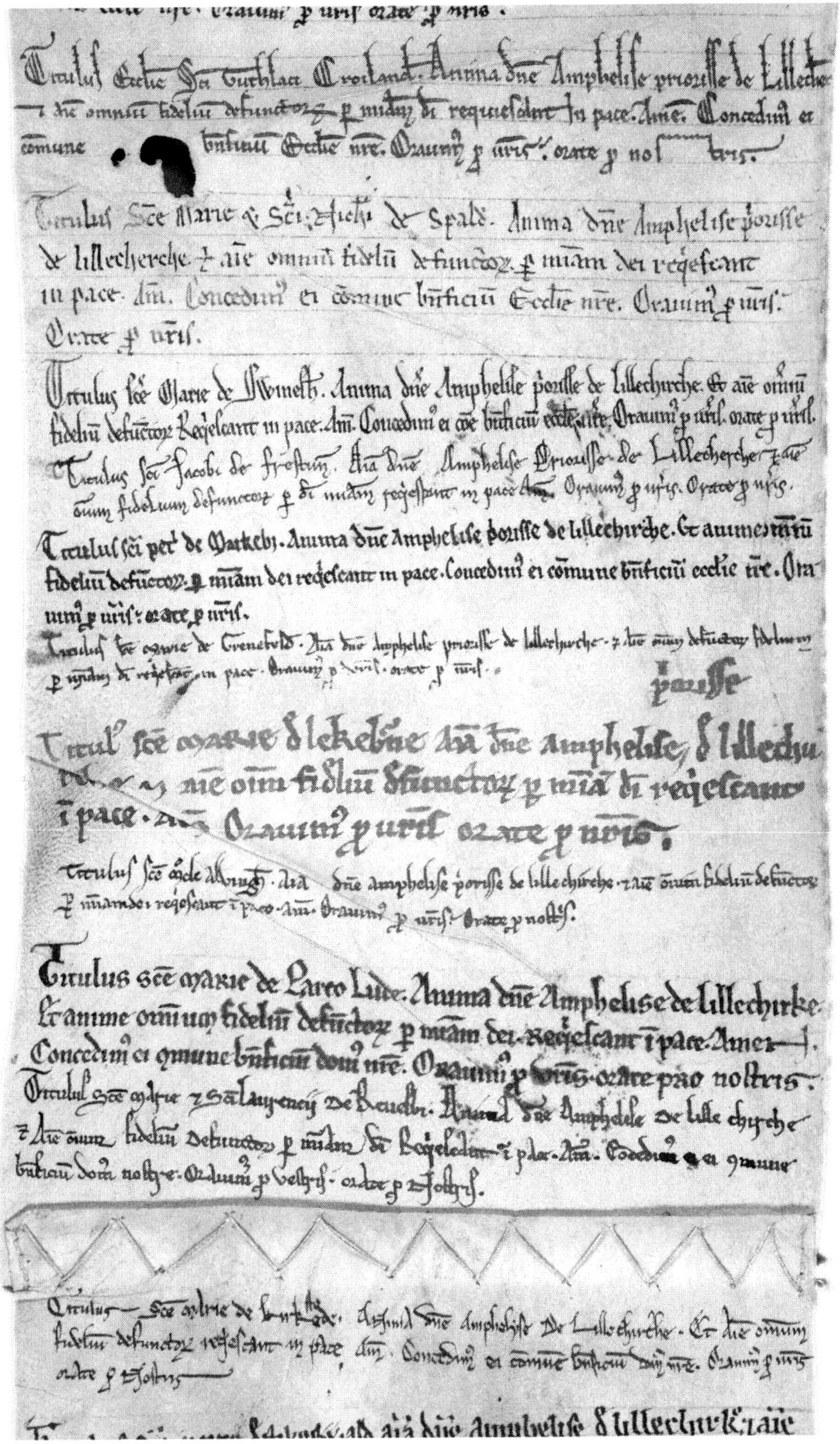

Figure 12. Amphelisa Roll, Cambridge, St. John's College, MS N. 31. By permission of the Master and Fellows of St. John's College, Cambridge. Photograph © Ian McKee.

frequent up-to-date palaeographical features in ca. 1215–1220 appear in our data. The number of different script-types here is notable, but so is the quality of the handwriting—some of it categorizable as regular, expert, and professional (as with the entry for *Parco Lude*, or Louth Park, towards the bottom) and some of it indicating scribes who, while trained, were surely not "professional" or, indeed, the most expert of craftspersons (the entry for Lekeburne or Legbourne Priory in the lighter brown ink, for example). Book hands, charter hands, and blended hands are all on display here simultaneously and contiguously, containing absolutely contemporary forms (barred capitals, crossed Tironian *notae*, straight abbreviation marks) and forms that had been around for some decades by this time (**d** with the high ligatured **e**, the *nota* descending below the line, and the Lombardic **T** opening the Louth Park *titulus*).

The variety in this mortuary roll is exemplary of the diversity of hands and scripts in the later twelfth and thirteenth centuries. That diversity led Sir Hilary Jenkinson to write *Palaeography and the Practical Study of Court Hand* in 1915.[4] In it, Jenkinson published thirteen plates with descriptions and evaluation, and these plates demonstrate how different scribal outcomes were. In a section at the back of the book, Jenkinson reveals the trick of the entire book: that all the plates show scripts written in the very same year, despite their extreme variation of hand. His motivation is, as he says, to show "that the importance of Palaeographical Science is overrated"; and "that a great deal of time is given unnecessarily to Palaeography."[5] His answer is to prioritize the history of administration, from which knowledge of dates and formulae can be better derived than through palaeography.

Palaeography has important work to do, though—despite Jenkinson's scepticism. Close and slow transcription and description of these Mortuary Rolls, and the use of digital tools to analyse the data, testifies to the multiple approaches and methods now available for studying the variation of scribal practices from the bottom up, as it were: inductively, without the superimposition of template of ideal scripts.[6] Emphatic doubts have been raised about the role of the digital environment in making progress in manuscript studies. In Professor David Ganz's obituary for Professor Malcolm Parkes, he stated:

---

4 Jenkinson, *Palaeography and the Practical Study*.

5 Jenkinson, *Palaeography and the Practical Study*, 36.

6 Doubts about the role of palaeography, because of its subjectivity, have been raised by other scholars. See Treharne, *Perceptions of Medieval Manuscripts*, especially Chapter 9.

> [Parkes's] work is a reminder that, in the age of digital palaeography and its supposedly scientific advances, there is no substitute for constant contact with manuscripts, and for an ability to do more than describe them. Tables of page sizes may enable us to distinguish books from different centres, but we are entitled to ask why a particular scribe or patron chose a particular format to copy a particular text. Sadly books are for reading, not just for looking at the scripts or the pictures.[7]

Modern palaeography need not be an either/or: a reading *or* a looking. It might be best served through a combination of methods—some tried and tested (close reading, transcription, first impressions) and some new (data training, algorithmic trials, visualization). The global pandemic in 2020–2023 reminded all scholars that without digital palaeography very few researchers would have been able to make any advances at all in their work with manuscripts if it were not for the digital repositories available freely. In this sense, then, the digital environment is the great equalizer.[8] It is as important an environment for textual critics, literary analysts, and linguistic researchers. To capitalize and exploit this richness of resource, scholarly training is more important than ever—in palaeography and other interpretative approaches that explain modes of textual production. Scholars can exploit digital possibilities, and indeed palaeography itself, as tools in a wider armoury that includes the assembly of rich textual and historical contextual evidence to build a broader interdisciplinary picture for medieval textual production.

Is palaeography (or historical linguistics, or medieval literary studies, or history) a field, a discipline, a *category*, that is prepared to question itself? Are these core areas of research and teaching prepared to make themselves accessible and open to both upcoming and established scholars who work on languages and traditions other than Latin, or whose credentials vary while their encouragement should not? Large-scale changes are afoot, from the development of ChatGPT and other AI models that permit rapid translation (that absolutely requires meticulous checking by trained scholars) to the possibilities that digitization permits for creating a more nuanced account of developments in the writing of manuscripts and documents, testing long-established foundational narratives. These new approaches, coupled with traditional slow scholarship, require open-mindedness and an acceptance that former published accounts might require modification; and

---

7 https://medievalfragments.wordpress.com/2013/06/06/malcolm-b-parkes-palaeographer-1930–2013/.

8 Yet digital tools and methods represent only two of the sixty-three chapters in Coulson and Babcock, *Oxford Handbook of Latin Palaeography*.

yet that there is so much invaluable earlier scholarship upon which others can and must build—but build openly and generously. Such open-mindedness extends particularly to premodern textual cultures and communities of writers. *Disrupting Categories* has, then, sought to contribute to this idea of exploration beyond categories: categories that allow for the neat parcelling up of time, literature, language, history, and script, but that also often close down more flexible or imaginative interpretative possibilities. The reappraisal of early texts beyond the edges of periods, disciplines, and taxonomies—edges invented by the academy to permit delineation for courses and (ultimately unrepresentative) tidiness—opens up a fresh set of opportunities for old and new scholars alike. There has never been a more urgent time than now to welcome new scholars, new techniques of analysis, and new explorations into the histories, forms, languages, and meanings of the human record. This arena of interdisciplinary humanities research stands to benefit significantly from different, innovative, and generous thinking. Such thinking will allow a broadening of our horizons, moving us beyond established categories of understanding to new possibilities that can be created by allowing our textual objects of study to speak for themselves.

BIBLIOGRAPHY

Aiello, Matthew. "English Vernacular Script in the Thirteenth Century (ca. 1175–ca. 1325)." *New Medieval Literatures* 21 (2021): 29–77.

Anderson, G. K. *The Literature of the Anglo-Saxons*. Princeton: Princeton University Press, 1949.

Assmann, Bruno, ed. *Angelsächsische Homilien und Heiligenleben*. Bibliothek der angelsächsischen Prosa 3. With supplement by P. Clemoes. Darmstadt: Wissenschaftliche Buchgesellschaft, 1964. First published in 1883 by Wigand: Kassel.

Atherton, Mark. "Cambridge, Corpus Christi College 201 as a Mirror for a Prince: *Apollonius of Tyre* Archbishop Wulfstan and King Cnut." *English Studies* 97 (2016): 451–72.

Bailey, Richard N. "St. Cuthbert's Relics: Some Neglected Evidence." In St. *Cuthbert: His Cult and His Community to A.D. 1200*. Edited by Gerald Bonner, Clare Stancliffe, and David Rollason, 231–46. Woodbridge: Boydell, 1989. Reprint, 1998.

Baker, Adam. "Arts and Humanities Cuts 'Endemic.'" *The Times Higher Education Supplement*, May, 2022.

Baker, Timothy M., and Beverly Kienzle. "Monastic Preaching and the Sermon in Medieval Latin Christendom to the Twelfth Century." In *The Cambridge History of Medieval Monasticism in the Latin West*. Edited by Alison Beach and Isabelle Cochelin, 710–28. Cambridge: Cambridge University Press, 2020.

Barlow, F. *English Episcopal Acta XI: Exeter 1046–1184*. Oxford: Oxford University Press, 1996.

Belfour, A. O., ed. *Twelfth-Century Homilies in MS. Bodley 343*. Early English Text Society, o.s., 118. London: Kegan Paul, 1909.

Betha Colaim Chille: Life of Colum Cille. Edited and translated by Andrew O'Kelleher and Gertrude Schoepperle Urbana: University of Illinois, 1918. Reprint Kessinger's Rare Reprints, 1994.

Bishop, T. A. M. "Notes on Cambridge Manuscripts: Part II." *Transactions of the Cambridge Bibliographical Society* II (1954–58): 185–99.

Blake, Norman, ed. *The Cambridge History of the English Language*. 2 vols. Cambridge: Cambridge University Press, 1992.

Borges, Jorge Luis. *La cifra*. Barcelona: Emece, 1981.

Borges, Jorge Luis, and María Kodama. *Breve Antología Anglosajona*. Santiago: Ediciones La Ciudad, 1978.

Breay, Claire. *Magna Carta: Manuscripts and Myths*. London: British Library, 2002.

——, and Harrison, Julian, eds. *Magna Carta: Law, Liberty, Legacy*. London: British Library, 2015.

Briggs, Elizabeth. "Religion, Society, and Politics, and the *Liber Vitae* of Durham." PhD diss, University of Leeds, 1987.

Browett, Rebecca. "The Fate of Anglo-Saxon Saints after the Norman Conquest of England: St. Æthelwold of Winchester as a Case Study." *History* (2016): 183–200.

Browett, Rebecca. "Touching the Holy: The Rise of Contact Relics in Medieval England." *Journal of Ecclesiastical History* 68, no. 3 (2017): 493–509.

Buchholz, Richard. *Die Fragmente der Reden der Seele an den Leichman*. Erlanger Beiträge 6. Leipzig: Erlangen, Leipzig, 1890.

Butler, Emily. *Language and Community in Early England: Imagining Distance in Medieval Literature*. New York: Routledge, 2017.

Butterfield, Ardis. "The Dream of Language: Chaucer 'en son Latin.'" *Studies in the Age of Chaucer* 41 (2019): 3–29.

Carpenter, David. "The Cartulary Copies at Lincoln and Salisbury of the Lincoln and Salisbury Engrossments of the 1215 Magna Carta," 2015; http://magnacarta.cmp.uea.ac.uk/read/feature_of_the_month/May_2015_2.

Carpenter, David. *Magna Carta*. London: Penguin, 2015.

Chaplais, Pierre. *English Royal Documents: King John-Henry VI (1199–1461)*. Oxford: Clarendon, 1972.

Clanchy, M. T. *From Memory to Written Record: England 1066–1307*. 3rd ed. Oxford: Wiley-Blackwell, 2013.

Clark, Cecily. *The Peterborough Chronicle 1070—1154*. Oxford: Clarendon, 1970.

Clayton, Mary, and Hugh Magennis, eds. *The Old English Lives of St. Margaret*. Cambridge Studies in Anglo-Saxon England 9. Cambridge: Cambridge University Press, 1994.

Clayton, Mary. *The Cult of the Virgin Mary in Anglo-Saxon England*. Cambridge Studies in Anglo-Saxon England 2. Cambridge: Cambridge University Press, 1990.

Cleaver, Laura. "Pages Covered with a Many Tears as Notes: Herbert of Bosham and the Glossed Manuscripts for Thomas Becket." In *Herbert of Bosham: A Medieval Polymath.* Edited by Michael Staunton, 232–44 Woodbridge: Boydell, 2019.

Clemoes, P., ed. *Ælfric's Catholic Homilies: The First Series: Text.* Early English Text Society, s.s., 17. London: Oxford University Press, 1997.

Collins, Arthur Jeffries. "The Documents of the Great Charter of 1215." *Proceedings of the British Academy* 34 (1948): 233–79.

Conlee, John W., ed. *Middle English Debate Poetry: A Critical Anthology*. East Lansing: Colleagues, 1992.

Constable, Giles. *Three Studies in Medieval Religious Thought: The Interpretation of Mary and Martha, The Ideal of the Imitation of Christ, The Orders of Society*. Cambridge: Cambridge University Press, 1995.

Conti, Aidan, "Individual Practice, Common Endeavour: Making a Manuscript and Community in the Second Half of the Twelfth Century." In *Producing and Using English Manuscripts in the Post-Conquest Period*. New Medieval Literatures 13. Edited by Orietta Da Rold, Mary Swan, and Elaine Treharne, 253–72. Turnhout: Brepols, 2012.

——. "Preaching Scripture and Apocrypha: A Previously Unidentified Homiliary in an Old English Manuscript, Oxford, Bodleian Library, MS Bodley 343." PhD diss., University of Toronto, 2004.

Conybeare, J. J. "Communication of an Inedited Fragment of Anglo-Saxon Poetry." *Archaeologia* 17 (1814): 1–5, 173–75.

Conybeare, W. D., ed. *Illustrations of Anglo-Saxon Poetry*. London: Harding, 1826.

Crane, Susan. "Anglo-Norman Cultures in England, 1066–1460." In *Cambridge History of Medieval Literature*. Edited by David Wallace, 35–60. Cambridge: Cambridge University Press, 1999.

Da Rold, Orietta. *Paper in Medieval England: From Pulp to Fictions*. Cambridge: Cambridge University Press, 2020.

——, Takako Kato, Mary Swan, and Elaine Treharne. *The Use and Production of English, 1060 to 1220*. University of Leicester and Stanford University, 2010, 2018. https://em1060.stanford.edu/.

Denholm-Young, N. *Handwriting in England and Wales*. Cardiff: University of Wales Press, 1957.

Derolez, Albert. *The Palaeography of Gothic Manuscript Books from the Twelfth to the Early Sixteenth Century*. Cambridge: Cambridge University Press, 2003.

Dictionary of Old English A to I Online. Edited byAngus Cameron et al. Toronto: Dictionary of Old English, 2018.

Djordjević, Ivana, Nicole Clifton, and Judith Weiss, trans. *Waldef: A French Romance from Medieval England*. Leeds: ARC Humanities, 2020.

Dronke, Peter, ed. *A History of Twelfth-Century Western Philosophy*. Cambridge: Cambridge University Press, 1988.

Duggan, Anne. "Master Herbert: Becket's *eruditus*, Envoy, Adviser, and Ghost-Writer." In *Herbert of Bosham: A Medieval Polymath*. Edited by Michael Staunton, 29–54. Woodbridge: Boydell 2019.

Edwards, Kathleen. *The Secular Cathedrals in the Middle Ages*. Mancheser: Manchester University Press, 1967.

Fafinski, Mateusz. *Roman Infrastructure in Early Medieval Britain*. Amsterdam: Amsterdam University Press, 2021.

Farge, Arlette. *The Allure of the Archive*. New Haven: Yale University Press, 2004.

Faulkner, Mark. *A New Literary History of the Long Twelfth Century*. Cambridge: Cambridge University Press, 2022.

Foucault, Michel. *The Order of Things: An Archaeology of the Human Sciences*. Translated by A. M. Sheridan. New York: Vintage, 1970.

Foucault, Michel. *The Archaeology of Knowledge*. Translated by A. M. Sheridan. New York: Pantheon, 1972.

Franklin, Carmen Vircillo. "The Reception of the Latin Life of St. Giles in Anglo-Saxon England." *Anglo-Saxon England* 42 (2013): 63–145.

Franzen, Christine. "On the Attribution of Additions in Oxford, Bodleian MS Bodley 343 to the Tremulous Hand of Worcester." *American Notes and Queries* 19 (2010): 7–8.

——. *The Tremulous Hand of Worcester: A Study of Old English in the Thirteenth Century*. Oxford: Clarendon, 1991.

Fulk, R. D., and C. Cain. *A History of Old English Literature*. Oxford: Wiley, 2005.

Furnivall, F. J., ed. *The Fifty Earliest English Wills in the Court of Probate, London*. Early English Text Society, o.s., 78. Oxford: Oxford University Press, 1882. Reprint, 1964.

Galbraith, V. H. "A Draft of Magna Carta (1215)." *Proceedings of the British Academy* 53 (1967): 345–60.

Gameson, R. "The Emergence of Formal Gothic Script in England." In *Oxford Handbook of Latin Palaeography*. Edited by Frank Coulson and Robert Babcock, 361–68. Oxford: Oxford University Press, 2020.

Geary, Patrick. *Phantoms of Remembrance: Memory and Oblivion at the End of the First Millennium*. Princeton: Princeton University Press, 1994.

Gilbert, Jane, and Miranda Griffin, eds. *The Futures of Medieval French: Essays in Honour of Sarah Kay*. Gallica. Cambridge: Brewer, 2021.

Godden, Malcolm. *Ælfric's Catholic Homilies: Introduction, Commentary and Glossary*.Early English Text Society, s.s., 18. Oxford: Oxford University Press, 2000.

——, ed. *Ælfric's Catholic Homilies, The Second Series: Text*. Early English Text Society, s.s., 5. Oxford: Oxford University Press, 1979.

Gray, Douglas. "Christina of Markyate: The Literary Background." In *Christina of Markyate: A Twelfth-Century Holy Woman*. Edited by Samuel Fanour and Henrietta Leyser, 12–24. London: Routledge, 2004.

Grieve, Hilda E. P. *Examples of English Handwriting, 1150–1750*. Colchester: Essex Record Office, 1954.

Gumbert, J. P. "Format of Books." In *Oxford Handbook of Latin Palaeography*. Edited by Frank Coulson and Robert Babcock, 633–43. Oxford: Oxford University Press, 2020.

Gutgsell, Jessie. "The Gift of Tears: Weeping in the Religious Imagination of Western Medieval Christianity." *Anglican Theological Review* 97, no. 2 (2014): 239–53.

Hahn, Thomas. "Early Middle English." In *The Cambridge History of Medieval English Literature*. Edited by David Wallace, 61–91. Cambridge: Cambridge University Press, 1999.

Hall, Thomas N. "The Earliest Anglo-Latin Text of the *Trinubium Annae* (BHL 505zl)." In *Via Crucis: Essays on Early Medieval Sources and Ideas in Memory of J. E. Cross*. Edited by Thomas N. Hall with Thomas D. Hill and Charles D. Wright, 104–37. Morgantown: West Virginia University Press, 2002.

Handley, Rima. "British Museum MS. Cotton Vespasian D. xiv." *Notes and Queries* 219 (1974): 243–50.

Hanna, Ralph. Review of *The Cambridge History of the Book in Britain: Volume II, 1100—1400*, edited by N. J. Morgan and R. M. Thomson. *Journal of English and Germanic Philology* 109 (2010): 389–94.

Harmer, Florence. *Anglo-Saxon Writs*. Manchester: Manchester University Press, 1952.

Hart, C. "The Codex Wintoniensis and the King's *Haligdom*." In *Land, Church and People: Essays Presented to Prof. H. P. R. Finberg*. Edited by J. Thirsk, 7–38. Reading: Museum of English Rural Life, 1970.

Hector, L. C. *The Handwriting of English Documents*. Dorking: Kohler, 1966.

Heller, Nathan. "The End of the English Major." *The New Yorker*, February, 2023. https://www.newyorker.com/magazine/2023/03/06/the-end-of-the-english-major.

Heng, Geraldine. *The Global Middle Ages: An Introduction, Cambridge Elements*. Cambridge: Cambridge University Press, 2021.

——. *The Invention of Race in the European Middle Ages*. Cambridge: Cambridge University Press, 2018.

Heningham, Eleanor K. "Old English Precursors of 'The Worcester Fragments." *Proceedings of the Modern Language Association* 55, no. 2 (1940): 291–307.

Hill, Joyce. "Two Micro-Texts in Ælfric's *Catholic Homilies*: A Puzzle Revisited." In *Anglo-Saxon Micro-Texts*. Edited by Ursula Lenker and Lucia Kornexl, 131–41. Berlin: De Gruyter, 2019.

Holt, J. C. *Magna Carta*. 3rd ed. Cambridge: Cambridge University Press, 2015.

——. *Magna Carta and Medieval Government*. London: Hambledon, 1985.

Home, Malasree. *The Peterborough Version of the Anglo-Saxon Chronicle: Rewriting Post-Conquest History*. Anglo-Saxon Studies 27. Woodbridge: Boydell, 2015.

Ihnat, Kati. "Early Evidence for the Cult of Anne in Twelfth-Century England." *Traditio* 69 (2014): 1–44.

Irvine, Susan. "The Compliation and Use of Manuscripts Containing Old English in the Twelfth Century." In *Rewriting Old English in the Twelfth Century*. Cambridge Studies in Anglo-Saxon England 30. Edited by Mary Swan and Elaine Treharne, 41–60. Cambridge: Cambridge University Press, 2000.

——. *Old English Homilies from MS Bodley 343*. Early English Text Society, o.s., 302. Oxford: Oxford University Press, 1993.

Jenkinson, Hilary. *Palaeography and the Practical Study of Court Hand*. Cambridge: Cambridge University Press, 1915.

Johnson, David F. "The Micro-Texts of the Tremulous Hand of Worcester: Genesis of a Vernacular *liber exemplorum*." In *Anglo-Saxon Micro-Texts*. Edited by Ursula Lenker and Lucia Kornexl, 255–66 (Berlin: De Gruyter, 2019).

Jones, Chris. "Re-lining *The Grave*: A Slow Reading of MS Bodley 343, fol. 170r." In *Slow Scholarship: Essays and Studies*. Edited by Catherine E. Karkov, 53–78. Woodbridge: Boydell, 2019.

Ker, Neil. *Catalogue of Manuscripts Containing Anglo-Saxon*. Oxford: Clarendon, 1957. Reprint, 1991.

——. "The Date of the 'Tremulous' Worcester Hand." In *Books, Collectors and Libraries: Studies in the Medieval Heritage*. Edited by Andrew G. Watson, 67–69. London: Hambledon, 1986.

——. *English Manuscripts in the Century after the Conquest*. The Lyell Lectures. Oxford: Clarendon, 1960.

Keynes, Simon. "Anglo-Saxon Charters Lost and Found." In *Myth, Rulership, Church and Charters: Essays in Honour of Nicholas Brookes*. Edited by Julia Barrow and Andrew Wareham, 45–66. Aldershot: Ashgate, 2008.

——. *The Liber Vitae of the New Minster and Hyde Abbey Winchester*. Early English Manuscripts in Facsimile 26. Copenhagen: Rosenkilde, 1996.

Kienzle, Beverley Mayne. "Exegesis on Luke 10:38 around 1100: Worcester MS F. 94, ff. 1r-2r, a Tribute to James E. Cross." *Medieval Sermon Studies* 40 (1997).

Kihlman, Erika, ed. *Expositiones sequentiarum: Medieval Sequence Commentaries and Prologues*. Stockholm: University of Stockholm Press, 2006.

——. "Medieval Sequence Commentaries." *Proceedings of the Fifth International Congress for Medieval Latin Studies*, 110–24. The Journal of Medieval Latin 17. Toronto: University of Toronto Press, 2006.

Kim, D. "Female Readers, Passion Devotion, and the History of MS Royal 17. A. xxvii." *Journal of the Early Book Society* (2015): 153–214.

Kitson, Peter. "Old English Dialects and the Stages of Transition to Middle English." *Folia Linguistica Historica* 11 (1992 for 1990): 27–87.

Kluge, Friedrich. *Angelsäschisches Lesebuch*. Halle: Niemeyer, 1897.

Lacey, Brian, ed. *Manus O'Donnell's Life of Colum Cille*. Dublin: Four Courts, 1998.

Lakoff, George. *Women, Fire, and Dangerous Things: What Categories Reveal about the Mind.* Chicago: Chicago University Press, 1987.

Laing, Margaret. *Catalogue of Sources for a Linguistic Atlas of Early Middle English.* Cambridge: Brewer, 1993.

Lass, Roger. *Old English: A Historical Linguistic Companion.* Cambridge: Cambridge University Press, 1994.

Lerer, Seth. "The Afterlife of Old English." In *The Cambridge History of Medieval Literature.* Edited by David Wallace, 7–34. Cambridge: Cambridge University Press, 1999.

Love, R. C. "St. Neot." In *Blackwell Encyclopaedia of Anglo-Saxon England.* Edited by Michael Lapidge, Simon Keynes, and Donald G. Scragg. Oxford: Wiley, 1999.

Machan, Tim William. *English in the Middle Ages.* Oxford: Oxford University Press, 2003.

McCully, Chris and Sharon Hilles. *The Earliest English: An Introduction to Old English Language.* London: Pearson, 2005.

Meehan, Bernard. "A Reconsideration of the Historical Works Associated with Symeon of Durham: Manuscripts, Texts and Influences." PhD diss, University of Edinburgh, 1979.

Miller, Sean, ed. *Charters of the New Minster, Winchester.* Anglo-Saxon Charters 9. Oxford: Oxford University Press, 2001.

Moffat, Douglas, ed. *The Soul's Address to the Body: The Worcester Fragments.* East Lansing: Colleagues Press, 1987.

Morgan, Edwin. "*The Grave.*" In *Dies Irae*, 39–40. Silver Lake: Lotus Press, 1952. Re-published in *Poems of Thirty Years.* Manchester: Carcanet, 1982.

Morris, Richard, ed. *Old English Homilies of the Twelfth Century from the Unique MS. B. 14. 52.* Early English Text Society, o.s., 53. London: Trübner, 1873.

Mynors, R. A. B., and R. M. Thomson. *Catalogue of the Manuscripts of Hereford Cathedral Library.* Cambridge: Brewer, 1993.

Nilson, Benjamin. *Cathedral Shrines of Medieval England.*Woodbridge: Boydell, 2001.

Ó hÓgáin, Dáíthí. "Migratory Legends in Medieval Irish Literature." *Bealoideas* 60–61 (1992/1993): 57–74.

Parkes, M. B. "Handwriting in English Books." In *Cambridge History of the Book in Britain.* Edited by N. J. Morgan and R. M. Thompson, 110–35. Vol 2. Cambridge: Cambridge University Press, 2008.

Parkes, M. B. *English Cursive Book Hands, 1250–1500.* Oxford: Clarendon, 1969.

Pelikan, Jaroslav. *The Christian Tradition: A History of the Development of Doctrine.* Volume 3 of *The Growth of Medieval Theology (600–1300).* Chicago: Chicago University Press, 1978.

Pfaff, Richard W. *The Liturgy in Medieval England: A History.* Cambridge: Cambridge University Press, 2008.

Plummer, Charles, ed. "Life of Maedoc of Ferns." In *Bethada Náem nÉrenn: Lives of Irish Saints, 177–83*, 177–83. Oxford: Oxford University Press, 1922.

Pope, J. C., ed. *Homilies of Ælfric: A Supplementary Collection.* Early English Text Society, o.s., 269, 260. London: Oxford University Press, 1967–1968.

Prescott, Andrew. "'Their Present Miserable State of Cremation': The Restoration of the Cotton Library. In *Sir Robert Cotton as Collector: Essays on an Early Stuart Lawyer and his Legacy.* Edited by C. J. Wright, 391–454. London: The British Library, 1997.

Radulescu, Raluca, and Sif Rikhardsdottir, eds. *Routledge Companion to Medieval English Literature*. London: Routledge, 2023.

Raine, James. *Saint Cuthbert: With an Account of the State in which His Remains Were Found upon the Opening of His Tomb in Durham Cathedral, in the Year MDCCCXXVII*. Durham: Andrews, 1828.

Rambaran-Olm, Mary. "A Wrinkle in Medieval Time: Ironing Out Issues Regarding Race, Temporality, and the Early English." *New Literary History* 52 (2021): 385–406.

Ramsay, Jennifer. "A Possible 'Tremulous Hand' addition to *The Grave* in MS Bodley 343." *Notes and Queries* 49, no. 2 (2002): 178–80.

Reginald of Durham. *Reginaldi Monachi Dunelmensis Libellus de Admirandis Beati Cuthberti Virtutibus*. Publications of the Surtees Society. London: Nichols, 1835.

Renevey, Denis. "Enclosed Desires: A Study of the Wooing Group." In *Mysticism and Spirituality in Medieval England*. Edited by William F. Pollard and Robert Boenig, 40–62. Cambridge: Brewer, 1997.

Rich Jones, W. H., ed. *Register of S. Osmund*. 2 vols. London: Longman, 1883.

Richards, Mary P. "On the Date and Provenance of the MS Cotton Vespasian D.XIV, ff. 4–169." *Manuscripta* 17 (1973): 31–35.

——. *Texts and Their Traditions in the Medieval Library of Rochester Cathedral Priory*. Transactions of the American Philosophical Association 78, no. 3. Philadelphia: American Philosophical Association, 1988.

Rieger, Max. *Alt- und Angelsächsisches Lesebuch: Nebst Altfriesischen Stücken; Mit Einem Wörterbuche*. Giessen: Ricker, 1861. Reprint, 2018.

Rigg, A. G. *A History of Anglo-Latin 1066–1422*. Cambridge: Cambridge University Press, 1992.

Rollason, David. "St. Cuthbert and Wessex: The Evidence of CCCC MS 183." In *St. Cuthbert: His Cult and His Community to A.D. 1200*. Edited by Gerald Bonner, Clare Stancliffe, and David Rollason, 413–24. Woodbridge: Boydell, 1989. Reprint 1998.

——, ed. and trans. *Symeon of Durham: Libellus de exordio atque procurso istius, hoc est Dunhelmensis, ecclesie*. Oxford Medieval Texts. Oxford: Oxford University Press, 2000.

Rowlands, I. W. "The Text and Distribution of the Writ for the Publication of Magna Carta, 1215." *English Historical Review* 124 (2009): 1422–31.

Rumble, Alexander R. *Property and Piety in Early Medieval Winchester: Documents Relating to the Topography of the Anglo-Saxon and Norman City and its Minsters*. The Anglo-Saxon Minsters of Winchester 3. Oxford: Clarendon, 2002.

——. "The Structure and Reliability of the *Codex Wintoniensis* (British Museum Additional MS 15350: the Cartulary of *Winchester* Cathedral Priory)." 2 vols. PhD diss., University of London, 1980.

Saltzman, Benjamin A. "Writing Friendship, Mourning the Friend in Late Anglo-Saxon *Rules of Confraternity*." *Journal of Medieval and Early Modern Studies* 41, no. 2 (2011): 251–91.

Sauer, Hans. "Knowledge of Old English in the Middle English Period?" In *Language History and Linguistic Modelling: A Festschrift for Jacek Fisiak on his 60th Birthday*. Trends in Linguistics 101. Edited by Raymond Hickey and Stanislaw Puppel, 791–814. Berlin: De Gruyter, 1997.

Saunders, W. *Ancient Handwritings*. London: Bernau, 1909.

Savage, Anne. "Old and Middle English: Poetry and Prose." *Studies in the Age of Chaucer* 23 (2001): 503–11.

Scase, Wendy. *Visible English: Graphic Culture, Scribal Practice, and Identity, c. 700–c. 1550*. Turnhout: Brepols, 2022.

Schroer, Arnold. "*The Grave*." *Anglia* 5 (1882): 289–90.

Scragg, D. G., ed. *The Vercelli Homilies and Related Texts*. Early English Text Society, o.s., 300. Oxford: Oxford University Press, 1992.

Short, Douglas D. "Aesthetics and Unpleasantness: Classical Rhetoric in the Medieval English Lyric Called *The Grave*." *Studia Neophilologia* 48 (1976): 291–99.

Short, Ian. "Language and Literature." In *A Companion to the Anglo-Norman World*. Edited by Christopher Harper-Bill and Elisabeth Van Houts, 191–213. Woodbridge: Boydell, 2003.

Siebert, Eve. "A Possible Source for the Addition to *The Grave*." *American Notes & Queries* 19, no. 4 (2006): 8–16.

Skeat, W. W., ed. *Ælfric's Lives of Saints*. Early English Text Society, o.s., 76, 82, 94, 114. London: Oxford University Press, 1889–1900. Reprint, 1966.

Southern, Richard, ed. and trans. *The Life of St. Anselm*. Oxford Medieval Texts. Oxford: Clarendon, 1962.

Stroud, Daphne. "Salisbury's Magna Carta: Was It Issued by the Chancery?" *The Hatcham Review* 2 (1981): 51–58.

Swan, Mary. "Old English Made New: One Catholic Homily and its Reuses." *Leeds Studies in English*, n.s. 28 (1997): 1–18.

——, and Elaine Treharne, ed. *Rewriting Old English in the Twelfth Century*. Cambridge Studies in Anglo-Saxon England 30. Cambridge: Cambridge University Press, 2000.

Tahkokallio, Jaakko. *The Anglo-Norman Historical Canon: Publishing and Manuscript Culture*. Cambridge Elements. Cambridge: Cambridge University Press, 2019.

Thacker, Alan. "St. Waerburh: The Multiple Identities of a Regional Saint." In *The Land of the English Kin: Studies in Wessex and Anglo-Saxon England in Honour of Professor Barbara Yorke*, 443–66. Leiden: Brill, 2020.

Thomson, R. M. *Catalogue of Manuscripts of Worcester Cathedral Library*. Woodbridge: Boydell, 1999.

Thorpe, Benjamin, ed. *Analecta Anglo-Saxonica: A Selection, in Prose and Verse, from Anglo-Saxon Authors of Various Ages*. London: Arch 1834.

——. *Diplomatarium Anglicum Aevi Saxonici: A Collection of English Charters*. 2 vols. London: Macmillan, 1865.

Treharne, Elaine. "The Dates and Origins of Three Twelfth-Century Manuscripts." In *Anglo-Saxon Manuscripts and Their Heritage: Tenth to Twelfth Centuries*. Edited by Philip Pulsiano and Elaine M. Treharne, 227–52. Aldershot: Ashgate, 1998.

——. "The Form and Function of the Old English *Dicts of Cato*." *Journal of English and Germanic Philology* 102, no. 4 (2003): 65–85.

——. "'The Good, the Bad, the Ugly': Old English Manuscripts and Their Physical Description." In *The Genesis of Books: Studies in the Scribal Culture of Medieval England in Honour of A. N. Doane*. Edited by Matthew Hussey and John Niles, 261–83. Turnhout: Brepols, 2012.

——. "The Life of English in the Mid-Twelfth Century: Ralph D'Escures's Homily on the Virgin Mary." In *Literature of the Reign of Henry II*. Edited by Ruth Kennedy and Simon Meecham-Jones, 169–86. London: Routledge, 2006.

——. *Living Through Conquest: The Politics of Early English 1020–1220*. Oxford: Oxford University Press, 2012.

——. *Medieval Literature: A Very Short Introduction*. Oxford: Oxford University Press, 2015.

——. "'Miserere, meidens': Abbesses and Nuns." In *Women and Medieval Literary Culture*. Edited by Corinne Saunders and Diane Watt, 27–49. Cambridge: Cambridge University Press, 2023.

——. "A Note on the Sensational Life of St. Margaret." In *Saints and Scholars: New Perspectives on Anglo-Saxon Literature and Culture in Honour of Hugh Magennis*. Edited by Stuart McWilliams, 5–13. Cambridge: Brewer, 2012.

——. *The Old English Life of St. Nicholas with the Old English Life of St. Giles*. Leeds: University of Leeds Press, 1997.

——. *Perceptions of Medieval Manuscripts: The Phenomenal Book*. Oxford: Oxford University Press, 2021.

——. "The Production and Script of Manuscripts Containing English Religious Texts in the First Half of the Twelfth Century." In *Rewriting Old English in the Twelfth Century*. Cambridge Studies in Anglo-Saxon England 30. Edited by Mary Swan and Elaine Treharne, 16–40. Cambridge: Cambridge University Press, 2000.

——. "'Terrible Letters': Bad Handwriting and its Consequences, 1020–1220." *SELIM* 28 (2023): 79–96.

——, and Mateusz Fafinski. *Medieval Networks of Memory*. Stanford: Stanford Text Technologies, 2023. https://medievalnetworks.github.io/mnm.

Underwood, Ted. *Why Literary Periods Mattered: Historical Contrast and the Prestige of English Studies*. Standford: Stanford University Press, 2013.

VanDyke Friedlander, Carolynn. "Early Middle English Accentual Verse." *Modern Philology* 76 (1978–9): 219–30.

Vincent, Nicholas. *Australia's Magna Carta*. Canberra: Commonwealth of Australia, 2010.

——. *Magna Carta: A Very Short Introduction*. Oxford: Oxford University Press, 2012.

——. "Why 1199? Bureaucracy and Enrolment under John and his Contemporaries." In *English Government in the Thirteenth Century*. Edited by Adrian Jobson, 17–48. Woodbridge: Boydell, 2004.

Wadsworth Longfellow, Henry. *Poems and Other Writings*. New York: Library of America, 2000.

Wallace, David, ed. *Cambridge History of Medieval Literature*. Cambridge: Cambridge University Press, 1999.

Ward, Bernard, ed. *The Life of St. Edmund, Archbishop of Canterbury*. St. Louis: Herder, 1903.

Warner, R. N. *Early English Homilies from the Twelfth-Century MS. Vesp. D. XIV*. Early English Text Society, o.s., 152. London: Oxford University Press, 1917 for 1915.

Weiskott, Eric. *English Alliterative Verse: Poetic Tradition and Literary History*. Cambridge: Cambridge University Press, 2016.

——. *Meter and Modernity in English Verse, 1350–1650*. Philadelphia: University of Pennsylvania Press, 2020.

Whitehead, Christiania. *The Afterlife of St. Cuthbert*. Cambridge: Cambridge University Press, 2020.

Wilcox, Jonathan. "Oxford, Bodleian Library, Bodley 343." In *Homilies by Ælfric and other Homilies*. Anglo-Saxon Manuscripts in Microfiche Facsimile 17. Edited by A. N. Doane and P. Pulsiano, 71–101. Tempe: Center for Medieval and Renaissance Studies, 2008.

Wilmart, A. "Les homélies attribuées à S. Anselme." *Archives d'histoire doctrinale et littéraire de moyen âge* 2 (1927): 5–29, 339–41.

Wogan-Browne, Jocelyn, ed. *Language and Culture in Medieval Britain: The French of England, c. 1100–c. 1500*. York: York Medieval, 2009.

Wright, C. E. *English Vernacular Hands from the Twelfth to the Fifteenth Centuries*. Oxford: Clarendon, 1960.

Wright, Charles D. *The Irish Tradition in Old English Literature*. Cambridge: Cambridge University Press, 1993.

Wright, David H. Review of "The Relics of St. Cuthbert," by C. F. Battiscombe. *The Art Bulletin* 43, no. 2 (1961): 141–60.

Yoshikawa, Naoe Kukita. "Veneration of Virgin Martyrs in Margery Kempe." In *Writing Religious Women: Female Spiritual and Textual Practices in Late Medieval England*. Edited by Christiania Whitehead and Denis Renevey, 177–95. Toronto: University of Toronto Press, 2000.

Younge, George. "The Canterbury Anthology: An Old English Manuscript in its Anglo-Norman Context." PhD diss., University of Cambridge, 2012.

——. "The New Heathens: Anti-Jewish Hostility in Early English Literature." In *Writing Europe, 500–1450*. Essays and Studies 68. Edited by O. Da Rold, A. Conti, and P. Shaw, 123–46. Cambridge: Brewer, 2015.

INDEX OF MANUSCRIPTS

GENERAL INDEX